HEART
OF A LEADER

MOSES

MIKE HILSON

Amanda Majerowicz, Editor
Emily Fussner, Cover & Layout Designer

I would like to dedicate this book to the numerous people who have invested in my understanding and practice of leadership. I could never properly mention them all, but let me say thank you to a few. Doug Helms who took a teenager with issues and invested time and insights into him. Dr. Harry Wood who found a struggling young pastor and saw leadership promise that no one else saw. Dr. Wayne Schmidt who took the time to explain his thinking and pray for a leader for whom he had high hopes. Dr. John Maxwell and Dr. Rick Warren who have been tremendous influences in my life from a distance. And ultimately, Dr. J. B. Hilson and Reverend Robert Freeman, my grandfathers, who as dedicated and committed Wesleyan pastors and leaders modeled for me what godly ministry and leadership should look like.

I thank God for you all.

CONTENTS

ACKNOWLEDGMENTS

I want to thank my wife, Tina, who has been my partner in life and ministry: I love you! To our three boys, Robert, Stephen, and Joshua, thank you for taking this journey of ministry with us and having a great attitude about it along the way. Also, thank you for growing up to be reliable, solid men I can count on and in whom I take great (hopefully godly) pride.

I want to sincerely thank my family at New Life Church for giving me the freedom to grow as a leader and follower of Christ.

Most importantly, I want to thank and praise God!

INTRODUCTION

FIVE LEVELS OF LEARNING AND LEADING

> *But when she could hide him no longer, she got a papyrus basket for him and coated it with tar and pitch. Then she placed the child in it and put it among the reeds along the bank of the Nile.*
>
> —*Exodus 2:3*

One of my areas of study, research, and teaching is that of leadership emergence patterns, theoretically known as leadership development theory. It forces you to look at a lifetime with long-range perspectives. When you step back and view a person's life history telescopically, you see things that you may otherwise miss.

—Dr. J. Robert Clinton, *The Making of a Leader*

The development of our leadership skills is a learning process. That process has been described in many ways through the years. While all of the patterns I have read have been helpful, I, like many other leaders I know, have developed a way of describing this process in my own mind. It makes sense to me. I think I can see it in my life and in the life of Moses. It's all about learning. The truth is that one cannot effectively lead without constantly learning. The world is rapidly changing and the process of rapid change is not going to stop as long as humans are involved. So we must be constantly learning and adapting if we are going to effectively lead. As we learn and adapt, we are taking a journey of development that will ultimately lead each of us to our area of greatest giftedness and fulfillment. We need to remember that fulfillment is the goal. Wealth, power, and fame are fleeting and cheating mistresses. But fulfillment, that's a life-giving partner. So, as we consider these, remember the goal and don't get knocked off track by things that just don't matter.

Here are the five stages of learning successful leadership:

1. **Learning to Be**

2. **Learning to Make a Difference**

3. **Learning to Give Direction**

4. **Learning to Build Structure**

5. **Learning to Leave a Movement**

Now, it should be stated from the outset that I don't think everyone will progress through all five levels. I actually think that each level is less populated than the previous one. While I believe that everyone must learn, and to some degree will learn, to be a friend, I have met only a handful of people who have given thought to the idea of learning to leave a movement. Therefore, there will be very few people who work on level five; everyone will work on level one. Remember, the levels are not achievement zones that we must pass through in order to be successful in life. They are simply areas of learning that help us develop into what God always meant for us. Some will read all five of these and find their sweet spot in level three. Others will find their hearts burning for level four. Some will find fulfillment in level two. There isn't better or best here, just different.

As we move forward, each level will be illustrated by a point in Moses' life and titled by a leadership phrase from my experience. These phrases are not brilliant. In fact, you may find some of them to be simple-minded. My goal is not to impress you with words or phrases; my goal is to establish a leadership language that can be accepted and used to facilitate the work that the Holy Spirit wants to do in each of you. So, don't take this journey expecting to be blown away by my intelligence, or expecting to be taught how everyone can and should move to level five. Take this journey seeking the best place for you to find the sweet spot of leadership God has for you. Look for progress that leads to fulfillment. Find the direction and permission to simply BE a *"fine child."*

LEARNING TO BE

> *Now a man of the tribe of Levi married a Levite woman, and she became pregnant and gave birth to a son. When she saw that he was a fine child, she hid him for three months.*
>
> *—Exodus 2:1-2*

In the long haul, God is preparing you for convergence. He is conforming you to the image of Christ (Romans 8:28-29), and He is giving you training and experience so that your gifts may be discovered. His goal is a Spirit-filled leader through whom the living Christ ministers, utilizing the leader's spiritual gifts. The fruit of the Spirit is the mark of the mature Christian. The gifts of the Spirit are a mark of a leader being used of God. God wants that balance. His approach is to work in you, and then through you.

—Dr. J. Robert Clinton, *The Making of a Leader*

God designed you to be you, and no one else!

One of my greatest joys is the privilege of leading people and empowering them in the calling that God has placed on their lives. I absolutely love watching as the Holy Spirit develops and then releases the energy that only He can put into a servant of His. As people who work for me or around me continually grow and improve, I am increasingly fulfilled through their work of becoming all who God created them to be.

However, leading and empowering people are two of the most frustrating things I do. Far too often, instead of celebrating the miraculous progress of someone finding and serving in the very center of their giftedness, I watch people struggle trying to serve in the area of someone else's giftedness. It is a far too common problem. In the book, *Spiritual Leadership*, the authors comment on a study conducted by George Barna and points out the very real struggle:

> George Barna conducted a survey of senior pastors from across various denominations. When asked if they believed they had the spiritual gift of leadership, only 6 percent responded yes. The fact that 94 percent of the senior pastors surveyed did not believe they were gifted to be leaders may explain the sense of desperation many church leaders express as they examine their ministry and its current effectiveness. (Blackaby 2001, 31)

This "sense of desperation" exists at every level of the church, and as far as I can tell, at every level of other organizations as well. It is a terribly frustrating thing to watch play out. I see two reasons for this problem.

Organizational Misplacement

I think that organizations (churches, corporations, governments, etc.) have a tendency to promote anyone who is doing well in their current position. On the surface, this makes sense. If a person is excelling at their current level of responsibility, give them more responsibility and let them excel at a higher level. Logical. Since most organizations increase salaries with increased levels of responsibilities, most people are more than happy, even excited, to take the "promotion."

What if it's not really a promotion? What if we are actually removing a person from their effective and successful work only to place them in an area for which they are not gifted? Increased levels of responsibility come with decreased levels of connection with the work that the employee was successful at in the beginning. When an organization takes someone who has excelled at, say, rug weaving and promotes them to manager of rug weavers, that employee gets a raise, a bigger office, and increased authority in the organization. They also are no longer weaving rugs. If fulfillment came from weaving rugs, then the pay raise, bigger office, and increased authority mean very little. In fact, at this point, the organization has not promoted this individual; they have enslaved them. Fulfillment is no longer a reality. The increased pay scale and the lack of effective paths to return to fulfilling work, leave this once effective and fulfilled artist frustrated and trapped. When this occurs, we have committed the old, proverbial sin of throwing a person into ever-deeper pools until we find out in which one they will drown.

Personal Misjudgment

This mistake is not solely a failure of organizations. In some organizations, leaders work hard to properly place people in areas of work that will bring the highest level of fulfillment. They try not to promote someone right out of their effectiveness and happiness. However, even when the organization is trying to get it right, the individual often gets it wrong. All too often, people want to be someone else. They can't be satisfied with their blessing. Instead, they want someone else's blessing, all the while not realizing that the person whose blessing they covet has secretly been coveting someone else's blessing, maybe even theirs!

It often looks like this in church circles. God is richly blessing His servant in a given area of ministry. Since the church seems to over-celebrate the communicating pastor, that servant decides he or she must become the primary communicator in the organization. However, God doesn't bless that work the way He blessed the other work. I have heard it so many times and it's more saddening than maddening. "But if I'm not the preacher on Sunday then I'm not the leader any other time." That doesn't have to be true. Far too often, the effectiveness and blessing of what one is doing now is obscured and ultimately shut down by the seemingly irresistible draw to the "top job."

What's the solution to this problem? We need to hear from God what Moses' mother instantly knew about her son. *"When she saw that he was a fine child"* (Exodus 2:2). God created you, and you are a *"fine child."* We must tear down our false ideas about importance and instead serve in the reality of God's economy. The rug weaver is a fine child of God. The manager of the rug weavers is a fine child of God. The custodian at the church is a fine child of God. The youth pastor at the church is a fine child of God. The small group leader, the community organizer, the fast-food worker, the truck driver, the CEO, the receptionist, the garbage collector, and the President are all fine children of God. We need to understand that there really is no best or better in areas and levels of service. There is just different. Yes, some pay more than others, and the variance can be dramatic! However, higher pay scales do not always speak to importance. When I shop at Wal-Mart, I assume that the highest paid person in the organization is the CEO. I don't know his name and I have never met him. Honestly, I don't care to, but Peggy who works as a cashier is important. I think she likely deserves a raise, but that's the CEO's decision, not mine. Her pay scale does not change the fact that, as far as I'm concerned, she is the most important person in the organization at the moment I check out with my disposable treasures.

We must stop trying to obtain someone else's blessing and honestly pursue the very best God has for us, regardless of society labels and levels. We must somehow learn to be a *"fine child"* of God and trust Him with the rest.

YOU ALWAYS HAVE A REASON

> *These are the names of the sons of Israel who went to Egypt with Jacob.*
>
> *—Exodus 1:1*

God knows what your life can become. Only He understands your full potential as His child. He does not want you to miss out on anything He has for you.

—Henry and Richard Blackaby, *Experiencing God*

There is an age-old question when it comes to great historical leaders. "Does the man (or woman) make the times or do the times make the man (or woman)?" This question, while interesting, likely misses the point that people and situations make each other. Men and women are formed from their surroundings, situations, cultures, families, events, and histories. Some may be defined or detained by such things while others learn to lead and influence. It is the latter who gain the opportunity to reshape their surroundings, situations, cultures, families, events, and futures. In his work, *The Making of a Leader*, Dr. J. Robert Clinton calls these formative years "Phase I" or the "Sovereign Foundations" stage of the leadership development. He describes this phase as the time where "God providentially works through family, environment, and historical events" to begin setting the stage for a leader's development" (Clinton 1988, 44).

In the life of Moses, as it is found in the biblical books of Exodus, Numbers, and Deuteronomy, we must consider how the nation of Israel got to the place that they needed a Moses. If you go back to the book of Genesis, you will find the roadmap that led to the environment into which Moses was born. By the time we get to chapter 42 of Genesis, a man named Jacob has twelve sons. Jacob is also known by another name, Israel. He is literally the father of the nation of Israel. His twelve sons will be the founders and, mostly, namesakes of the twelve tribes of Israel. One of his sons is named Joseph. He is his father's favorite, and therefore his brother's least favorite. His brothers, in fact, hate him so deeply that they sell him into slavery and tell their father that a wild animal killed him. Through a very complex and difficult series of really tough events, Joseph finally ends up in direct service to the Pharaoh of Egypt. By God's design, Joseph has journeyed from slavery to being the second in command of the nation of Egypt. (This journey from slave to power is at the core of Moses' story as well!) Joseph's job is to prepare for a great famine that God has told him is coming. When the famine arrives, it threatens to kill everyone, including Joseph's family, the children of Israel. The Bible says at this point: *"When Jacob learned that there was grain in Egypt, he said to his sons, 'Why do you just keep looking at each other?' He continued, 'I have heard that there is grain in Egypt. Go down there and buy some for us, so that we may live and not die'"* (Genesis 42:1-2).

Jacob and his sons have no idea that Joseph is in charge of the grain in Egypt. Through a long process of discovery and slow revelation, they realize that the brother they rejected has become the savior they need. (There is so much here we are going to pass over!) There is no food or water in their land, their promised land, and so Joseph speaks to Pharaoh and asks if his family can stay in Egypt. *"Pharaoh said to Joseph, 'Your father and your brothers have come to you, and the land of Egypt is before you; settle your father and your brothers in the best part of the land. Let them live in Goshen'"* (Genesis 47:5-6).

Egypt, the nation that for Moses is wrongly holding his people as slaves, did not start out as a place of captivity. It started out as a place of refuge. A place of comfort. A land of plenty. *"The best part of the land."* However, by the time we get to the book of Exodus, things have changed:

> *Then a new king, to whom Joseph meant nothing, came to power in Egypt. "Look," he said to his people, "the Israelites have become far too numerous for us. Come we must deal shrewdly with them or they will become even more numerous and, if war breaks out, will join our enemies, fight against us and leave the country." So they put slave masters over them to oppress them with forced labor.* (Exodus 1:8-11)

What started out as a place of refuge and comfort ultimately became a place of bondage and destruction. Unfortunately, this is a very common story. Many people have retreated to a safe, comfortable, *"best"* place in an attempt to escape pain, anguish, hurt, anger, and failure. After a while, that place of comfort becomes a place of captivity.

And so it was with the children of Israel. The place where they found refuge has now become a prison. Why? The answer is really quite simple. While the land of Goshen inside the borders of Egypt was a great place, it wasn't their place. They did not belong there. It was fine for them to find refuge there for a time, and even some peace and enjoyment there for a time. It just wasn't where God wanted them to be. In the book, *Good to Great*, the author begins with the simple adage, "Good is the enemy of great" (Collins 2001, 1). The story of Moses is made necessary by the failure of the children of Israel to remember that God had promised them another land. God had promised a land even better than the one they currently occupied, *"a land flowing with milk and honey"* (Exodus 3:17). They had settled for good when God promised them great, and now good had gone bad.

Moses is born into this bad situation. His life journey will begin and continue in danger, struggle, confusion, faith, strength, and miracle. All of this is part of God's plan for this great leader. The same is going to be true, at least to some extent, in your life. Your times will shape you. They are the canvas you are given to begin the work of art that will be your life journey. You cannot, no matter how much you want to, start anywhere else. These are your times. It is important that you not become depressed, defeated, or cynical. While it may seem that you have randomly been dealt a bad hand in life, the truth is far different. God has a plan. We will see in the life of Moses times when he is confused, lost, fearful, and just downright wrong.

The entire journey is marked by one inescapable truth; God is with him. And God is with you as well. You, like Moses, likely did not cause the problem you are now charged with fixing. However, you are nonetheless charged with fixing it! You don't make the times into which you are born, but you can affect the times you leave behind. This is the great story of Moses. He was handed a gathering of slaves large enough to be a nation. In one lifetime, he took that ragtag group of people who had never been anything but slaves, and built them into a nation that sparked fear into the hearts of every foe they faced.

Pretty impressive!

What about you? When you are feeling discouraged or depressed, consider the words that were spoken to another Old Testament hero. Her name was Esther. She found herself at the very center of power, the queen in fact, and at a moment when a madman named Haman wanted to destroy all the children of Israel. (This is a disturbingly common historical theme!) Her uncle Mordecai encouraged her with words I want you to hear. As Esther wrestled with the fact that revealing herself as a Hebrew and asking for mercy for her people could literally get her killed, Mordecai reminded her, *"And who knows but that you have come to your royal position for such a time as this?"* (Esther 4:14).

So your times may not be all that you wished and may be worse than you can imagine. But who knows! Perhaps God has made you, skilled you, built you, equipped you, and sent you specifically for such a time as this.

GOD ALWAYS HAS A PLAN

> *Now a man of the tribe of Levi married a Levite woman, and she became pregnant and gave birth to a son.*
>
> *—Exodus 2:1-2*

The story of Moses begins well before his birth. For decades prior, forces had been at work that would shape Moses into a faithful servant, forces directed by a sovereign hand — God's, not Pharaoh's.

—Stephen J. Lennox, *Moses: Faithful Servant of God*

God always has a plan.

In the darkest of moments when the skies seem bleak and barren and heaven seems hemmed in by the impenetrable dark clouds of hopelessness and despair, God is still at work. As the children of Israel are languishing under the harsh hand of a domineering king (who thinks he is a god), it must seem that God is oblivious to their plight. They must wonder to themselves as the lashes come down from their Egyptian overlords if God even sees them or even remembers them. We must remember that they are very far removed from the time of Joseph. *"Now the length of time the Israelite people lived in Egypt was 430 years"* (Exodus 12:40). Not only had the Pharaoh forgotten about the blessing that these Hebrew people had been to the

13

nation, the Israelites themselves must have been wondering if all those old stories actually held any truth. Perhaps God didn't really care about them after all?

It is in those dark moments that God is at work. "God was not absent from this chapter, though the circumstances seem to indicate otherwise…. He is ultimately responsible for the remarkable population growth among the Israelites, a growth rate the Egyptians were powerless to slow" (Lennox 2016, 22-23). In these dark days, God was preparing a nation to leave its bondage. A single family had moved to Goshen in Egypt. Now, over 400 years later, a nation had developed from that family. God had predicted that. And now that nation must be persuaded to leave the only place they had ever known as home and go to a land for which they would have to work and fight. God had a plan, but He needed to convince a nation that the plan was what they needed to accomplish. In the book, *The Heart of Change*, the authors begin with this simple truth: "People change what they do less because they are given *analysis* that shifts their *thinking* than because they are *shown* a truth that influences their *feelings*" (Kotter and Cohen 2002, 1). As we enter in to the story of Moses' life, God has already built this family, the children of a man named Israel (Jacob), into a nation. Their population growth rate is so large that it frightens the Egyptian King (Exodus 1: 8-22). Now God must convince the children of Israel that where they are is not where they need to be. Honestly, slavery and forced labor are great motivators for change. So, while it seems that God has forgotten His people, nothing could be farther from the truth!

God always has a plan.

Think about it. On the day that Moses' parents were married, no one noticed. The forced labor continued. No new cry of deliverance or light of hope dawned. No fear sparked in the heart of the Egyptian King. It was just like it had always been; yet, something very profound was taking place. God was working in the quiet relationship between two descendants of Levi the Priest. Next thing you know, a son is born. Again, there was no holiday or national celebration at the birth of Moses. In fact, his mother kept the fact that she had given birth to a son a strict secret. Pharaoh had issued a requirement that all boys born to Hebrew women were to be thrown into the river Nile (Exodus 1:22). So Moses' birth is only partly a joyous occasion. It was also a fearful occasion. Moses' mother knew of Pharaoh's order, and she knew she could only keep her son's birth a secret for a short time. At some point, she was going to have to put this child into the Nile or her entire family might pay the ultimate price for breaking the law of the Pharaoh. So it seems that nothing has changed. It seems that God is still ignoring the plight of His people. It seems that nothing will deliver Moses' family from the death sentence that has been placed on the tiny boy who they already love so much.

But God always has a plan.

The problem is we don't always want to trust God's plan.

LEARNING TO BE A FRIEND

> *Greater love has no one than this: to lay down one's life for one's friends.*
>
> —*John 15:13*

Today I see my purpose as adding value to others. It has become the focus of my life, and anyone who knows me understands how important it is to me. However, to *add value* to others, one must first *value* others.

—John C. Maxwell
Everyone Communicates, Few Connect

This is the most basic of leadership levels. It has been said that the key element to personhood is community. We all need and desire community. Real, transparent, honest, safe community. That community requires some things of us. It requires that we understand and value the people around us. It requires that we value others above ourselves. It requires that we are willing to *"lay down one's life for one's friends."* This admonition from Jesus was literally lived out by Him as He died on a cross for the salvation of the world. Now, in our reality, such drastic sacrifice may not be physically necessary. However, it will be emotionally necessary. All deep relationships are based in mutual submission. If we cannot voluntarily choose to surrender our self-interest for the interest of those around us, we will find it virtually impossible to build lasting, deep, transparent, and safe relationships and communities.

The ability to mutually submit for the betterment of others is normally first taught in the community of immediate family. At home, with those we live with and love, we should find ourselves most able to surrender our will for the betterment of those around us. As spouses, parents, children, whatever our role, we must be able to set aside our preferences in favor of the preferences of others. The beautiful thing is that when we live in an atmosphere of mutual submission, those in our family are also working to submit their preferences for the betterment of our preferences! When it works right, the result is beautiful.

Those who know our family well has virtually stopped asking me what our plans are after church or after some event where Tina (my wife) and I are together. They already know my response: "Wherever Tina is, I will be sitting beside her." What they don't know is that Tina will always look at me and say, "What do you want to do?" The truth is that most of the time I just don't care enough about where we eat or what we do to have an opinion. So she decides, and I sit next to her. On the occasion that I do have a preference, Tina will set aside her plans and let me choose. Either way, every time, we both strive to consider the other first. This is the way a good relationship works. Each party choosing to submit to the situation that is best for the other. While we may first learn this at home, if we are wise, we will learn to practice it to an appropriate level everywhere. Nobody actually cares how smart, rich, strong, popular, powerful, or famous you are, unless and until they know that you care about them. Then, well, they still don't care how smart, rich, strong, popular, powerful, or famous you are. The difference is this time they don't care because they like you anyway!

So, level one — learning to be a friend starts at home.

CONNECTIONS ONLY TAKE YOU SO FAR ... FAMILY IS FOREVER!

> *When the child [Moses] grew older, she [Moses' mother] took him to Pharaoh's daughter and he became her son. She named him Moses, saying, "I drew him out of the water."*
>
> —*Exodus 2:10*

Leaving the place of his youth, Moses goes out (va-yeitzei) to his kinfolk (2:11). He leaves behind the comfort of the palace to see his brothers and sisters, and in so doing not only changes his life, but will change the life of his people.... What seems to drive Moses is an intense desire to connect with his brothers and sisters.

—Norman J. Cohen
Moses and the Journey to Leadership

When Moses' mother handed him over to the Pharaoh's daughter, it must have been heartbreaking for both of them. She could have never known that God would one day bring this child back to her people. She no doubt thought that once having tasted the "good life" in the palace, her son would forget his heritage and abandon his people. This *"fine child"* she birthed was now going to become part of the unjust system that enslaved her and her people.

But that isn't how the story went.

It's true that Moses was raised in the palace of the very King who had decreed his death. The Pharaoh who demanded that everyone, like Moses, be drowned in the Nile (effectively sacrificing them to one of the Egyptian gods), would now give shelter, food, fine clothing, and the best education known to mankind to a child he had attempted to kill. Moses grows up with all the best things and all the best connections. By the time Moses is a grown man, he is connected to all the people that matter in society. He has power by his mere proximity to power. He has everything that a young man could possibly want.

But that isn't how the story went.

Moses knew he had the best of everything, but somehow he also knew he didn't belong there. He knew who his people really were and knew where they were. It seems possible that Moses may have never been allowed to forget he was Hebrew. It seems plausible to believe that on the playgrounds of the Egyptian palace's educational system, the other rich and well-connected kids could see that he was different, and they likely pointed that out. Moses could see he was different. Though Scripture does not tell us any of this, it is obvious that Moses yearned for some type of connection with the people outside the palace, his people. In the book, *Moses and the Journey to Leadership*, the author says, "Moses is not blinded by the wealth and power of his surroundings. He is able to truly see the enslaved Hebrews as his brothers and sisters" (Cohen 2007, 9).

Moses was somehow not fully connected with the family of his childhood. Instead, he is oddly connected with the real family of his birth.

This is how the story went.

The truth is that we all need some of this Moses trait in us. We all need to remember that family is ultimately what matters. Now, I am personally talking about actual blood-related family. I also understand that there are those in my life, and in yours, who are just as much family even though they are not blood-related. Whether your family is from birth or forged in the crucible of life, it is family that matters. Connections are important and absolutely essential in order to accomplish anything to which you have set your mind. However, in the end, it is family that will still be around when all of the connections are gone.

Early in my ministry, I was faced with what, at the time, felt like a devastating blow to my future. I was crushed, and I was away from home. My wife was caught in her work, and I felt very alone. At the time, my oldest son was around two years old. As my wife and I worked at this event where I experienced this crushing blow, my son was at the home of my in-laws. In my devastated, emotional state, I said to my wife, "I have to leave for a day or two. I can't stay." She asked me, "What are you going to do?" My response felt weak to me, but it was honest: "I'm going to get Robert and take a nap." When she asked me why, I responded, "Because no matter what these people think of me, my boy loves me." So I went home, gathered up my son who greeted me with that wonderful run toward me in excitement that just refilled my soul, and we took a nap. The next day, I was ready to go back and face what no longer seemed like the end of everything.

What made the difference?

Family made the difference. You see, eventually the connections break and the positions are lost. Eventually the job is over and the money just doesn't seem as important. The popularity wanes and the coolness that was once you, gives way to old man shoes and early dinners. When all of that happens, family is what's left. In fact, family is all that is left.

Therefore, as we do the work of climbing the ladders to significance, we should always keep family first. If family is all who's going to be there or all that's going to matter in the end, then quite frankly it should take the seat of importance throughout the process. In my life, I was fortunate enough to be taught this early. As I watched my mom family's stand by one another and always take care of one another, I learned that family must be central throughout life. And so, I have involved my family in every step of my career. Though we have accomplished more than most in our field, my wife and I have done it together and with our kids. While doing all of this, we have remained connected with our families. The simple truth is that the simple things are what will remain and ultimately matter. Too many people leave family in their wake as they chase fame, fortune, success, and power. Instead, we must be people who remember what is actually important and keep the main thing the main thing for the main portion of the time!

Moses may have been raised with the rich and powerful Egyptians ... but he belonged with the poor, hard-working Hebrews ... and he didn't let the trappings of wealth and power steal from him the beauty of birth and belonging.

Family matters ... act like it.

PRAYER BEFORE PASSION

> *One day, after Moses had grown up, he went out to where his own people were and watched them at their hard labor. He saw an Egyptian beating a Hebrew, one of his own people. Looking this way and that and seeing no one, he killed the Egyptian and hid him in the sand.*
>
> *—Exodus 2:11-15*

It seems that his [Moses] zealotry—his uncompromising commitment to his values and his preparedness to act decisively on those values—is the reason God chose him.

—Zvi Grumet, *Moses and the Path to Leadership*

People admire passion. People will follow those who show great passion. Passion really does matter. But passion must be kept under control.

Passion is a lot like fire. Fire is a good thing when it is handled properly. It gives us energy, warmth, it allows us to cook our food, and power our cars. Fire is a good thing, but fire must be kept under control. Uncontrolled fire is a disaster. Wildfires kill animals, destroy habitats, destroy homes, and kill people. Uncontrolled fire is not a force for good; it is a source of destruction. And passion is the same way. When we allow our passions to play out without control and thoughtfulness, we destroy lives and relationships. We can sink entire careers, and sometimes companies or movements, with uncontrolled passion. Passion is absolutely necessary but must be kept under control.

Passion is most often born in the midst of our closest relationships. Inside our families or among our closest friends, we establish the basis of what we want to see change in our world or in our lives. That passion then plays out into our personal reality and into the reality of those around us. Our passions drive our choices, our choices drive our direction, and our direction determines our destination. And sometimes, even in the midst of operating in our area of greatest passion, we make grave mistakes. When we operate in uncontrolled passion, we run the risk of losing the very relationships that birthed the passion in us. Our very stability can be undermined by our own choices. In the words of one writer, "A leader without self-control is unpredictable and dangerous." (Dilenschneider 2000, 74). Eventually that dangerous unpredictability will have grave consequences on everyone around the leader, including, and perhaps especially, those he loves most. "These losses of control on Moses' part had consequences even he could not foresee. Fleeing into the wilderness after killing the Egyptian, Moses became an outcast. Whereas he was once part of a community, now he couldn't even join his parents and siblings and his people, the Hebrew slaves, with whom he belonged." (Dilenschneider 2000, 73). Moses' loss of control or use of uncontrolled passion took from him everything he knew and everything he cared about.

Let's not miss one huge fact. Moses had every right to be angry with that Egyptian slave master. His reaction was righteous and in some ways heroic.

But he didn't do the right thing.

When we read this particular section of Scripture, there is something missing that is very common in Moses' older life. Prayer. Moses had a burst of anger, which sparked an idea and he took the time to consider *("Looking this way and that and seeing no one")*. He then he acted out of pure passion. No prayer. No thought. No consideration of consequences. Just passion, action, and destruction. An Egyptian lost his life. Moses lost his place and family. And the Hebrew slaves lost their best shot at an advocate in the palace. Destruction.

Even righteous passions can have devastating results if they are not handled properly. Prayer is the key to self-control in our lives. Prayer slows us down. It causes us to talk things out with God and listen to how we sound. When we pray to God and listen to our own words, we can catch ourselves being petty or impulsive. We can discover the dangers in our chosen path of action and perhaps even choose to change the pathway, so that we can avoid the destructive side of our choices while maximizing the positive side of our choices. Taking time to pray is key in our ability to exercise the self-control necessary to actually lead. In fact, this self-control is required even to maintain our relationships. Remember that Moses was driven away from all of his connections in the palace and his family in the Hebrew slaves. His relationships were ruined by his uncontrolled passion. For the next forty years of his life, he will live in exile from all that God had created him to do.

Later in Moses' life, he is described this way: *"The LORD would speak to Moses face to face, as one speaks to a friend. Then Moses would return to the camp"* (Exodus 33:11). With maturity came self-control. His passions were not lessened by life and age; his maturity was heightened and so his wisdom prevailed over his passion. While a young man, Moses acted out of pure passion and messed up everything. As a mature man, Moses prayed and waited to hear from God and then returned to the camp to take action. This maturity is what we need to control our passion. Hear me clearly; our passions are not a bad thing. It's when they are allowed to run unchecked by wisdom that they cause destruction. The Bible says that Moses spoke with God, *"face to face, as one speaks to a friend."* Where do you get that kind of prayer life? With time, and lots of it. Friends talk freely and bluntly with one another. But that freedom was not always there. When friends first meet, they are only acquaintances. As acquaintances, we don't have the freedom to be blunt and direct. Our words are more carefully chosen and our conversations more intentionally shallow. Over time, over years, over decades, we develop a level of trust and transparency that allows for real and intimate conversation to occur. This is the relationship that Moses has developed with God. It took time. I am not faulting

Moses for not having that deep, mature prayer life with God when he was a young man. I really doubt that would have even been possible, but he could have been trying.

Many of us struggle with this area of our lives, and the reason is really quite simple. God is still just an acquaintance. We don't really know Him the way we do our closest and dearest friends. The reason is that we haven't put in the time to get to know Him. We haven't spent the steady stream of hours and days wrestling with God, His word, and His presence. All of that is needed in order for us to clearly understand what He desires our next steps to be. We want to come to church and let the pastor speak God's word to us from the stage rather than do the work of digging out God's word from our own personal prayer closet. The simple fact is that we need to grow up. We need to mature. When we mature in our relationship with God, and the Holy Spirit can speak with us constantly and clearly, we will find in Him the ability to exercise wise self-control over the righteous passions of our heart. And when we do it God's way, we get to stay home.

ADMIT FAILURE QUICKLY AND PAY THE PRICE WILLINGLY

> *When Pharaoh heard of this, he tried to kill Moses, but Moses fled from Pharaoh and went to live in Midian.*
>
> —**Exodus 2:15**

Confession and forgiveness are precisely the disciplines by which spiritualization and carnality can be avoided and true incarnation lived. Through confession, the dark powers are taken out of their carnal isolation, brought into the light, and made visible to the community. Through forgiveness, they are disarmed and dispelled and a new integration between body and spirit is made possible.

—Henri J. M. Nouwen, *In the Name of Jesus*

We will all make our fair share of mistakes when we are young, and some of them will be devastating. In fact, we will make our fair share of mistakes, though hopefully less, when we are older too. Moses does not stop reacting in uncontrolled anger; he just does it far less often and repents immediately. That is the subject of this lesson. We are all going to mess up. Just deal with it. Just get past it, accept it, and move on. What needs to change in our lives is how we react to the discovery that we have messed up.

In our culture, there is an aversion to taking responsibility for our own failures. We have become a society of victims. Most in our culture would rather be the victim of someone else's bad choices or flawed heart than to admit that we actually caused our own failings. Rather than admitting our failure, we will simply find someone else to blame for it. We have fallen into the habit of statements like this: "It wasn't really my fault because that other guy ..." We blame strangers, government, neighbors, parents, genetics, weather, and God. We fail to take personal responsibility, and that leaves us broken.

Without confession, there cannot be correction. If I simply blame my failings on someone else, then I will make the false assumption that getting the other person out of the way will make what I did this time work next time. Then I just fall into a pattern of failure. Stinking thinking takes over and I end up wallowing in my own habitual bad choices. However, when that failure is acknowledged and repentance happens, then healing can begin to take place. Healing can make us much better leaders. "Failure is a powerful force in the making of a leader. The failure itself is not the issue; it's what the failure leads to that is so determinative in leadership development. For true leaders, failure will not destroy them but will, instead, further develop their character" (Blackaby 2001, 38).

But there is another step to this. Confession is necessary to bring light to the darkness of our failures. There is still going to be a price to pay. Although the ultimate price of our sin — an eternity separated from God — Christ paid on the cross of Calvary. There are still consequences. Actions always have consequences. The consequences of good, smart, godly actions are called blessings. They tend to make our lives better and our conscious clearer. The consequences of wrong, selfish, and sinful actions are not blessings at all. These consequences are dark and painful. Often times, the consequences of our personal actions can have destructive ramifications on innocent people around us. These consequences are not blessings; they are curses. But the price must still be paid. So we are left with two choices.

We can pay the consequences of our actions willingly and submissively.

We can pay the consequences of our actions begrudgingly and belligerently.

Please note that either way, we pay. There is no getting around the consequences of our actions. They are there like a pile of unattended trash that stinks and draws flies. It's clear to everyone that we have this decaying matter around us, but somehow we want to lash out and claim that someone else put that pile of rotten trash there! All the while, we know that the putrid mess is ours.

On this note, the young Moses seems to have handled himself fairly well. Granted, when the King wants to kill you, there tends to be a limited number of options for you to consider. Scripture gives us no indication that Moses at any point took the attitude of a victim. He seems to have understood his failure and left for Midian to pay his price. Biblical scholars have noted that there is very little information given to us concerning the next 40 years of Moses' life. What takes place for the next 40 or more years in his life and why do we not hear anything from him? Consider this compelling thought from one writer, Zvi Grumet:

> Indeed, it appears that following his killing of the Egyptian, Moses begins to recoil from his own actions. He looks in the mirror and does not like what he sees — a man so deeply passionate about his values that he kills for them. At first, the pullback involves replacing violent actions with challenging words. But then he removes himself completely from the scene and ends up as a shepherd — completely distanced from dealing with the problems of society or confronting the injustice to his own people. As one writer suggests, "the murder and subsequent flight are politically unproductive," yet the process of fleeing from Egypt and settling in Midian is transformative. Moses understands this, and being self-aware enough to realize that witnessing injustice will impel him to respond in ways he does not like, he retreats from public life and possibly even from most human interaction. (Grumet 2014, 32)

While our consequences may not be as dramatic as what Moses faced, and while it is likely not wise for us to retreat from "most human interaction," there will be a transformative effect brought on by our willingness to confess and pay the price for our failures. This transformation occurs in us as we take the time to process what caused these failures and put in place a plan to avoid their recurrence. Yet, the transformation does not stop there. God will take our humble confession and our willing submission and use it in a transformative way in the lives of those around us. It is in Midian that God does the work of preparing Moses for what will become his life's purpose; therefore, it is in Midian where the deliverance of God's nation of Israel begins.

2

LEARNING TO MAKE
A DIFFERENCE

Moses fled from Pharaoh and went to live in Midian, where he sat down by a well.

—Exodus 2:15

One of the greatest dangers associated with spiritual power is seen in those who exercise it without first having experienced God's transforming power. These religious power brokers know all the power plays; they are masters of rules, rituals, and organizational power games. But they lack the humility and brokenness necessary to enter into both an intimate relationship with God and loving relationships with others — a danger Jesus regularly confronted in the lives of the Pharisees, the religiously powerful of His day.

—Wayne Schmidt, *Power Plays*

Most people want to make a real difference in this world. Therefore, the burning question for leaders is not one of desire. The question is one of capacity. By capacity, I am only partly speaking of inborn talent. Everyone is born with talent. The talent we are born with is perfectly placed and balanced within

39

us for the accomplishment of all God has planned. Honestly, if we believe our own theology, it would help us here. I teach this to my congregation constantly, so let me do it here as well. It goes something like this:

Pastor: If you agree with what I am saying, say Amen! God created us all.

People: Amen!

Pastor: God created you specifically.

People: Amen!

Pastor: God created you for a reason.

People: Amen!

Pastor: God gifted you to accomplish what He created you for.

People: Amen!

Pastor: Therefore you already have everything you need to accomplish everything you were created to accomplish.

People: Amen!

Hopefully you were saying Amen as you read through that. You see, our theology teaches us of a Designer God who creates and empowers with purpose and meaning. Therefore, the conversation about capacity is only partly about inborn talent. That is there by God's design. The question is mostly about trying to bring that inborn talent out — discovering and developing it. In order for that to happen, God has to have our full attention.

Through the years, I have worked with many young pastors. None of them lacked talent. Some had more public talents than others, but all of them had talent. The difference between them was how deeply surrendered they were to the process of learning to use that talent for God's glory, and not their own. Those who are absolutely committed to building the Kingdom of God, no matter what the personal cost or who gets the professional credit, have always excelled. Those who were overly concerned about their own career or credit tended not to do so well. Congregations are made of people. People are looking for someone to help them change their lives, so that they can find God's best for them. Honestly, church folks can smell a self-centered fake who just wants to build his career at their expense a mile away. They won't follow that leader. The leader's abilities and talents may impress them, but they won't follow him. God has got to take us and make us into people who have learned to make a meaningful difference in the lives of others. He has got to break us down so that what shines through is His Word, His direction, and His Spirit. When our impressiveness gets in the way, people can't see God because of us. Our ego can become so large that it blocks out the light of the Son. When that happens, God must change us. Unfortunately, God often must break us.

Moses was raised in the palace and afforded the best education available. He walked the halls of power and held positions of authority. All of this, he has done in a very short period of time. Moses has also, impressively, not forgotten who he is. His people are not palace people, and he knows that. He has experienced hurt and anger as he saw the mistreatment of his people at the hands of the Egyptians. But Moses made a common, critical mistake for successful young leaders. He thought he could handle it his way, so he killed an Egyptian and almost got killed himself. Now, he sits at a well in Midian wondering what his next step is going to be. Likely confused and certainly in need. In one day, he has gone from a private room in the palace to being homeless sitting at the local watering hole. In his mind, he's done. It's over. His life peaked really early and now there is only the work of figuring out how to survive. He has reached the end.

What he doesn't realize is that this horrible moment is a great turning point in God's ultimate plan to prepare this young failure to become one of history's greatest leaders. Before God can truly use a great leader, He must prepare that leader to be committed to making a difference in others. God is not interested in making something great out of you. Although, that's what we would often prefer. God is interested in doing something great for others through you. He wants to empower you to make a difference. Before He can do that, He has to get your attention so that you can learn to hear His voice. He wants you to learn to care about others and desire to help others. He is going to put you in the perfect place to get that done. In the book, *Moses and the Journey to Leadership*, the author gives us an excellent explanation of how God is preparing Moses:

> Throughout the literature of the Ancient Near East and later, the role of the shepherd symbolizes leadership. People are often compared to a flock or a herd, and shepherding is considered a training ground for those destined to lead. There are numerous references in the Bible to leaders who were shepherds in their early lives; for example, King David. The Rabbis stress that Moses gains the necessary experience to redeem Israel and lead the people to the Promised Land precisely because he has been leading Jethro's flock in the wilderness. Moses is deemed the "faithful shepherd," who will deliver the People of Israel. (Cohen 2007, 16)

This new phase that Moses is entering is crucial for his development into the world-class leader God intends him to be. It may seem like a step down, but it's a step up. It may seem like a place of failure, but it's actually a place of future.

This is not the end … it is the beginning!

SEEK OUT CREATIVE BOREDOM

> *Now a priest of Midian had seven daughters, and they came to draw water and fill the troughs to water their father's flock. Some shepherds came along and drove them away, but Moses got up and came to their rescue and watered their flock. When the girls returned to Reuel their father, he asked them, "Why have you returned so early today?" They answered, "An Egyptian rescued us from the shepherds. He even drew water for us and watered the flock." "And where is he?" Reuel asked his daughters. "Why did you leave him? Invite him to have something to eat." Moses agreed to stay with the man, who gave his daughter Zipporah to Moses in marriage. Zipporah gave birth to a son, and Moses named him Gershom, saying, "I have become a foreigner in a foreign land."*
>
> *—Exodus 2:16-22*

Through the discipline of contemplative prayer, Christian leaders have to learn to listen again and again to the voice of love and to find there the wisdom and courage to address whatever issue presents itself to them. Dealing with burning issues without being rooted in a deep personal relationship with God easily leads to divisiveness because, before we know it, our sense of self is caught up in our opinion about a given subject. But when we are securely rooted in personal intimacy with the source of life, it will be possible to remain flexible without being relativistic, convinced without being rigid, willing to confront without being offensive, gentle and forgiving without being soft, and true witnesses without being manipulative.

—Henri J. M. Nouwen, *In the Name of Jesus*

Here is Moses' new reality — he married the preacher's daughter and became a shepherd. Not exactly what the young prince must have foreseen in his future from the vantage point of the Pharaoh's palace. But this is exactly where God needed him at this time in his development. Camping in the fields with no one to talk to except sheep and God, Moses was able to, perhaps for the first time in his life, be quiet. He had all the time in the world. No palace duties. No royal schooling. No leadership position. It was just sheep, God, and time. And while he must have despised the boredom of it, it was absolutely necessary for his development.

It seems that many of God's leaders have a desert experience somewhere in their lives — a time when they are unseen, unappreciated, unattached, and seemingly unused. Even Jesus was sent out into the desert to be tempted by Satan (Matthew 4:1-11, Mark 1:12-13, Luke 4:1-13). It is in these quiet and often boring times when God does the work of developing our capacity to think, to listen, to hear Him, and to devise ways and strategies that could have been used in a previous life phase, or could be used in a future one. All leaders need this kind of space in their world, yet few of them have it. Leaders are busy people. They became leaders because they worked hard and could be trusted. The more they lead effectively, the more people load on them. I have often noticed that the more effective or long-lasting my leadership at my church becomes, the more people push authority on to my desk. These days, after being the pastor here for nearly 20 years, I spend a lot of my time pushing authority on to someone else's desk. I need to do this. It is imperative that I have some empty space in my world. It is necessary for me to have what I have always termed as creative boredom.

The phrase creative boredom was birthed in my life when I was a teen. I didn't have a lot of friends and spent many hours wandering around our house in the country, down the creek and through the woods. I did a lot of thinking. I would do my chores and think. I would walk the creek and think. I would hike paths in the woods and think. I would sit alone, bored, and think. At the time, this seemed like some kind of private hell I couldn't escape. Looking back, all that thinking paid off. When I took my first solo pastor job, it all happened again. No one shows up at a small church during the week, except the pastor. I spent hours alone in that church building reading, writing, and thinking. At the time, I felt like I had somehow revisited that private hell from my teenage life. I was unnoticed, unheard, unthought-of, and seemingly unused by God. But none of that was true. Those hours of reading, thinking, and praying were priceless. They allowed me to develop ways of seeing the world and managing what I thought one day might be the reality in our church. I took the time to answer not just the "how" questions that are so common when everything is moving and shaking, but the "why" questions that seem to only get pondered when everything else stops moving. I had the time to find my voice on all kinds of issues.

Answering the "why" questions are really a process of finding your own unique voice on situations in life. This is imperative in the life of a leader. Finding the "whys" will inform and shape the "hows" in your life. But it takes time. It takes time that can seem unproductive. Quiet time. Down time. As one writer put it, "To find your voice, you have to explore your inner self. You have to discover what you care about, what defines you, and what makes you who you are. You can be authentic only when you lead according to the principles that matter most to you. Otherwise you're just putting on an act" (Kouzes and Posner 2012, 46). The good news is that once you have found your voice and figured out your "whys," those truths don't tend to change over time. For this reason, the "why" questions in your life are best dealt with in the beginning. They will give shape and meaning to all you do and all you decide. They will give purpose and stamina for a long and difficult journey. "Whys" give focus while your "hows" change constantly. Your "whys" will remain firm and unshaken, if you have defined them. If you don't take the time to define them early, one day you will be stumped when you look at the huge and growing challenges around you and find yourself asking "Why?" The question on this end of the equation will lead you to quit. "Why am I doing this anyway?" However, if you have effectively answered this exact question in the beginning, then your why does not lead you to quit. It gives meaning and purpose to the mounting "hows" that demand an ever-increasing amount of your time and energy. On that same day with all the pressure mounting, you may still ask yourself, "Why am I doing this anyway?" The difference is you will have an answer! The answer you will have will be the one you discovered in a lonely, forgotten, boring field surrounded by sheep … and God!

WHEN GOD SPEAKS ... LISTEN!

> *Now Moses was tending the flock of Jethro his father-in-law, the priest of Midian, and he led the flock to the far side of the wilderness and came to Horeb, the mountain of God. There the angel of the LORD appeared to him in flames of fire from within a bush. Moses saw that though the bush was on fire it did not burn up. So Moses thought, "I will go over and see this strange sight—why the bush does not burn up." When the LORD saw that he had gone over to look, God called to him from within the bush, "Moses! Moses!" And Moses said, "Here I am." "Do not come any closer," God said. "Take off your sandals, for the place where you are standing is holy ground." Then he said, "I am the God of your father, the God of Abraham, the God of Isaac and the God of Jacob." At this, Moses hid his face, because he was afraid to look at God.*
>
> *—Exodus 3:1-6*

The marvelous sight that Moses "sees" is not merely a lowly bush burning, but rather the awesome presence of God. What distinguishes leaders from followers is their ability to discern the impact of even simple events and actions.

—Norman J. Cohen
Moses and the Journey to Leadership

God speaks to His people. This is an absolute fact. The question is, do we hear Him?

In the life of a believer, it is the voice of God that ultimately answers the "why" questions we were wrestling with in our times of creative boredom. To be honest, without the intervening voice of God, creative boredom is mostly just boring and not really that creative at all. As leaders, we must learn to hear the voice of God clearly. In order to do that, we must recognize the presence of God quickly. I believe that in this account from Moses' life, we can find a process that will be helpful as we learn to hear from God in our own lives.

Wait for the timing of God

Moses has been in the desert for a long time. While I might have thought that my periods of creative boredom were long, I have nothing on Moses! It seems that Moses has served his father-in-law for forty or more years by the time we get to this encounter with God. Forty years before Moses can move on! Why so long? Well, we could make assumptions about what Moses was learning and what God was preparing back in Egypt, but in reality we don't know. Timing is in the hands of God. He is the one who knows everything about everything. If anyone were going to do everything at the right time, it would be God. It's not like God hasn't been working the entire time. In the book, *Experiencing God,* the authors put it this way: "God was already at work around Moses' life when He encountered

Moses at the burning bush. God had a purpose He was steadily working out in Moses' world. Even though Moses was an exile in the desert, he was right on God's schedule, in the fullness of God's timing, in the middle or God's will for that moment" (Blackaby et al. 2008, 54). This particular moment in Moses' life is significant for a reason that can be easily missed. Moses took the plight of the Israelites into his own hands as a young man and tried to set them free in his timing (not God's timing), and it almost killed him. Now, more than 40 years later, God is ready, and so is Moses, though he doesn't realize it yet.

Go to the mountain of God

Simply put, when you have an idea of where the power of God's spirit is moving, go there and hang out! I have heard many people pray that God would bless what they are doing. The problem with this prayer is that often what they are doing is a long way from what God is blessing. These folks are asking God to bless a program or style of ministry that was effective in a past generation. God did bless that. Now He is blessing something else. The logical choice for any leader would be to start doing what God is blessing, and the reason is very simple. If what I really want is God's moving and His will, then I am going to look for Him. When I find Him, I am going to go hang out where He is. If I hang out where He is, then I am going to be able to do what He is already blessing. That is so much easier than trying to convince Him to bless something just because you are doing it.

"But my heart is sincere and I just want God to be praised!" Really? If your heart is sincerely centered on God and all you want is for Him to be praised, then does it really matter what or who He is blessing? When the power of God is exhibited through anything, even a lowly unimportant scrub bush, then you should take notice and get close. If you refuse to approach the burning bush because you are too busy maintaining the ancient altar, you are going to miss standing on holy ground. Why would you do that? Well, it's actually not because of a sincere heart. It's actually due to arrogance. When you insist that God blesses in your way, on your timetable, or using your program, you have placed your ideas above God's will. That is arrogant. Surrender. And go hang out around the burning bush.

Look for the presence of God

The account tells us that Moses thought, *"I will go over and see this strange sight—why the bush does not burn up"* (Exodus 3:3). Moses was paying attention. "Moses only comes to appreciate the significance of the fire in the midst of the bush because he turns aside to look at the marvelous sight. First he has to see the bush aflame. He has to raise his eyes from the mundane desert sands and look to see" (Cohen 2007, 18). I believe that God will make sure we at least catch a glimpse of what He is doing around us. The rest is going to be up to us. Moses caught a glimpse of a bush on fire. This was likely not a completely unusual phenomenon in the desert. However, he noticed that something was different. He didn't simply shrug his shoulders and go back to cleaning up the park with his sheep pooper-scooper. He looked into it. I think a great deal of us miss wonderful opportunities because we are so busy watching sheep that we forget to take the time to watch for God. Then when the miraculous does come into our view, we kind of shrug our shoulders and say, "Well, that was odd." What we ought to do is get as close to that "marvelous sight" as we possibly can. We need to take the time to inspect a possible miraculous move of God. These moments don't happen all the time. When they do happen, we should slow down enough to check them out. The moment might just be life changing.

Listen for the voice of God

I have often been in meetings and in places where it was obvious that the Holy Spirit was moving and working. Whenever I enter into a moment like that, I will make myself internally stop all of my thinking and studying of my surroundings. I will force myself to just listen. That isn't always easy for me. I am naturally rather scattered and focus is not always easy to attain. Add to that the fact that these moments often come during church services or events. Being a pastor, I am busy surveying the crowd to assess their level of involvement, watching the stage to assess the management approach to the service, listening carefully to the music to see if the cut was in the right place or the drum beat was producing the desired effect during the build, or checking the room to see that it's clean, safe, and well maintained.... You're getting the picture, right? Focus isn't easy for me. However, when the Holy Spirit is moving, it is imperative that I make everything within me stop and listen. If I will do this, then I can often hear from the Lord in remarkable ways. God desires to speak to His people; we just don't always desire to listen. We are too busy serving Him to listen to Him, and that is too bad. The author of *Experiencing God* says, "God will draw you into a deeper and closer walk with Him so you can trust Him and have faith in Him. He will reveal His purposes to you so you can become involved in His work rather than merely pursuing your own goals and dreams" (Blackaby et al. 2008, 57).

Submit to the holiness of God

Now the final step before the big reveal: *"Take off your sandals, for the place where you are standing is holy ground"* (Exodus 3:5).

> As Moses approached the burning bush, God called to him from within it but forbade Moses to come closer and commanded him to remove his shoes (Ex. 3:4-5). In this same way, too, God taught Moses an important lesson: although too holy for casual access, God makes himself available to the humble. God would not allow his holiness to be taken for granted, but he graciously allowed his servant to come near. God also demonstrated his ability to sanctify any place. In the ancient Near East, the wilderness was seen as

an unholy place, but even that became holy ground when God was present. An ordinary bush became extraordinary by God's presence, and an unholy place was sanctified. Once Moses demonstrated his submission to God by removing his sandals, God revealed his identity. (Lennox 2016, 38)

That description captures my understanding of the holiness of this moment between God and Moses. The failed leader turned shepherd is now invited into the very presence of the Almighty. His responsibility in the moment is simple: surrender. Submit yourself in humility to the All Powerful God of Heaven. When we approach His presence with humility and surrender, He reveals Himself.

God speaks to His people. This is an absolute fact.

The question is, do we hear Him?

NO MINISTRY WITHOUT A MINISTER

> *The LORD said, "I have indeed seen the misery of my people in Egypt. I have heard them crying out because of their slave drivers, and I am concerned about their suffering. So I have come down to rescue them from the hand of the Egyptians and to bring them up out of that land into a good and spacious land, a land flowing with milk and honey—the home of the Canaanites, Hittites, Amorites, Perizzites, Hivites and Jebusites. And now the cry of the Israelites has reached me, and I have seen the way the Egyptians are oppressing them. So now, go. I am sending you to Pharaoh to bring my people the Israelites out of Egypt."*
>
> *—Exodus 3:7-10*

Nowhere is Moses's recoil more apparent than in his encounter at the Burning Bush and its aftermath. When God presents Moses with the plight of the Israelites in Egypt, Moses is notably disinterested in either the problem or in being part of the solution. The passionate man who earlier leapt into action, smiting an Egyptian or chasing away offensive Midianite shepherds, has apparently retired from public life — it is simply too painful to be involved and to have to control the rage which will inevitably be provoked…. In a word, Moses simply does not want to be involved. Ultimately, God rages at him, and instead of asking, commands him. Moses has no choice but to go.

—Zvi Grumet, *Moses and the Path to Leadership*

I must admit when I first read Zvi Grumet's take on Moses' reaction to the call of God at the burning bush, I was a little shocked. I had never seen Moses as "disinterested" in the suffering of the Israelites. I mean he killed an Egyptian and lost everything out of his concern for them. I always just thought that Moses was afraid. Then I thought it through. Moses had sincerely tried to do something about the mistreatment of his people as a young man, and, honestly, God didn't have his back. It must have seemed to Moses like, "Hey, I gave it my best shot and God didn't come through. Not going through that again." What Moses would have struggled with here is understanding that the problem wasn't with God's willingness to have Moses' back; the problem was Moses didn't take the time to understand God's plan and timeline. This event occurs again in the New Testament. When the guards sent from the Chief Priest arrest Jesus, the apostles are ready to fight for him, especially Peter. In all four of the Gospels, the account is retold. Peter, who had promised he would die for Jesus, draws his sword and cuts off the ear of one of the temple guards. Peter boldly demonstrates that he is prepared to keep his promise, and Jesus sternly rebukes his actions. Jesus heals the man who has come to arrest him! Can you imagine the confusion among the disciples? As a younger Christian, I was sometimes a little angry with the disciples for abandoning Jesus that night and not being visibly around when He was crucified. Then I unpacked this encounter with the guards and began to understand that they were confused. "If we can't defend you, what do we do? Just watch you die?" And so, they disappear until a meeting held three days later. Perhaps Moses is just having such a moment: Afraid of his own passions, confused by God's timing, and, honestly, pretty comfortable in the nice, simple, little life he has found as a shepherd. Moses cares about the people, but not enough to disrupt his own world.

But God is having none of that!

I think in our lives as leaders, we can often get confused and frustrated at God's will and timing. We can even get to the point that we love the Lord and we love the Church, but we just are no longer willing to disrupt our lives to do this "will of God" thing anymore. We haven't had any success discerning what His will is so far, and there just doesn't seem to be any good reason to think this time is any different.

But God is having none of that!

We have a phrase at the church I pastor that goes like this, "There is no ministry until there is a minister." The concept within our church is actually quite simple. I have watched too many pastors stress over finding leaders for ministries that no one wants to lead. In fact, the first church I served in full-time, there was a ministry leadership problem I had to deal with at the ripe old age of 23. The women's ministry leader decided she had done the job long enough, so she stepped down. We began to ask the other ladies in the group if they would be interested in leading. They all said no. Finally one of the new ladies in the church gave in and agreed to lead the women's ministry. In those days, in the Wesleyan Church, it was known as the Women's Missionary Society. So this new believer was now in charge of women's ministry and missions. I suppose it would have all worked out fine, except that the older ladies didn't like the way she was doing it. They would complain to her and each other about what she was doing. This went on for a while until that poor woman just walked in and quit. Hurt and confused, she didn't want to serve in the church anyone. I was ticked off. So I went to the Senior Pastor and made him an offer. I was leaving to take a solo pastorate in a few months anyway. I suggested that I would go in, shut the women's ministry down entirely, and take the heat for the decision. And there was going to be heat. I wanted the change for many reasons. I was tired of missions being viewed as "women's work" in our denomination. (An unintended consequence of this well-intentioned name choice perhaps a century ago.) I didn't want another lady in our church to be discouraged. He agreed and I shut it down. A few years passed and I was in another town pastoring another church when that pastor and I spoke about the women's ministry. He told me that one of the long-term ladies of the church had eventually come to miss the women's ministry. So she approached the pastor to ask permission to restart one. Having already started a missions' ministry with male and female leadership, he was able to separate missions from the woman's ministry and allow her to start the women's ministry afresh. This time, there was humility and passion in the leadership, and they had the strongest women's ministry in the history of the church.

I tell that story to illustrate two struggles we commonly face in church leadership.

1. "Somebody ought to do that but I just can't!"

Whether due to hurt, exhaustion, or disinterest, we often find that people just don't want to serve. Perhaps they are like Moses and feel that they have tried before but "God just didn't bless it," so they refuse to try again. Perhaps they are just too comfortable in their current schedule to disrupt their lives with ministry leadership. Perhaps they are just obstinate. It doesn't really matter why they won't step up; it matters that we don't force them. If God wants to "rage at them" and "command" them to do this thing, then the Holy Spirit will take care of that. As pastors and leaders in the church, we can't do the work of the Holy Spirit like that. We need to be willing to let a ministry cease to exist or not be established in the first place without leadership. While this may seem harsh and you may fear the backlash of people who demand that the ministry go on or be established, you just can't have effective ministry without called leaders. Honestly, if you pressure or guilt them into it, you are only going to end up with a sour, rotten ministry. It's just not worth it if there isn't called and surrendered leadership. So, if there is no minister, there is no ministry.

2. "This ministry is so important that this church can't exist without it!"

Now, here is one I really love! Some folks think that the ministry they lead is the central driving force of the entire church. They are wrong. Don't hear me wrong here. Ministries and leaders are important, but the only thing the church needs to carry on is worship and the Word. Those things don't require professional leadership to get done. Honestly, we are all replaceable. I was recently having a conversation with a pastor on our staff who each year has a conversation with me about retirement. He does not want to retire, but he doesn't want to overstay his usefulness either. So I said this to him: "You know that this church will continue to function without you or me. But having said that, it is my belief that at this stage in our church life, you are needed. So I am going to say the church needs you. I want you to stay at it!" And he did. Understanding that our service in the church is a privilege and not a right is imperative for pastors and volunteers.

There are other benefits to this leadership policy. When this is your policy, it helps you manage everyone else's great idea. There is rarely a shortage of great ideas that someone else should get accomplished! When people come to one of us and declare that they have the greatest idea for a ministry or they have discovered an area of service that is missing, our response is pretty standard. We do not promise to go find someone to create or lead this new ministry initiative. Instead, we simply look at the person with the idea and say, "You know, if the Holy Spirit it talking to you about this need, then that likely means you are the one He is calling to lead it." That simple approach will diminish your flow of "great ideas for others" by 90 percent. Once people are convinced that if the Holy Spirit is showing them the problem then He is likely calling them to address it, they get a lot more like Moses: "No, I think I'm good here watching sheep." If God truly is calling them, then He won't leave them alone till they follow. He will command them to move forward, and we won't have to force them. Furthermore, if someone is truly called to a ministry, we won't have grumpy leaders; we will have a Moses.

It's simple! No ministry without a minister.

ALLOW GOD'S STRENGTH TO OVERCOME MY WEAKNESS

> *Moses answered, "What if they do not believe me or listen to me and say, 'The LORD did not appear to you'?" Then the LORD said to him, "What is that in your hand?" "A staff," he replied. The LORD said, "Throw it on the ground." Moses threw it on the ground and it became a snake, and he ran from it. Then the LORD said to him, "Reach out your hand and take it by the tail." So Moses reached out and took hold of the snake and it turned back into a staff in his hand. "This," said the LORD, "is so that they may believe that the LORD, the God of their fathers—the God of Abraham, the God of Isaac and the God of Jacob—has appeared to you."*
>
> *—Exodus 4:1-5*

Although childhood experiences, physical strength, failures, successes, and even birth order can impact general leadership abilities, there is an added dimension to the growth of a spiritual leader that is not found in secular leadership development. That dimension is the active work of the Holy Spirit in leaders' lives.

—Henry and Richard Blackaby
Spiritual Leadership

When God told Moses to go back to Egypt and free His people, Moses was full of excuses. "I'm the wrong guy! Who do I say you are? They won't believe me. I don't talk well! Please, just send someone else!" There are many possible reasons for Moses to be so full of excuses. It's possible that to Zvi Grumet's point, Moses was just not interested in taking up this challenge. He may have soured on the entire idea of being the leader who would set the Hebrew people free. He, at the very least, had decided that his moment had passed. Then this Angel of the Lord from a burning bush shows up and wants to mess up his whole world? Perhaps he was too comfortable, too established in Midian to really desire any move back to the never-ending, busyness of life in Egypt. Either of these could be possible. I think the real answer is simpler than that. I think Moses felt inadequate for the task. Honestly, he was inadequate for the task.

And so are you.

Leadership within the church is similar to leadership in the world. It is also different. In the secular world, there are limits to what people can do. They can only do that of which they are capable. When a person in the secular world reaches the lid to his or her leadership skills, they must be replaced with someone who has a higher lid (capacity). Now, this same rule plays out in Christian leadership sometimes too. There is a caveat, a secret weapon that Christian leaders have that sets them apart: God.

When God calls a person to a task, He always calls them to something they cannot do. God desires to exhibit His power through His people. "God wants both to channel His power to us and to exercise His transforming power within us. But God's power play in the arena of the self doesn't end there. He does not intend for His power to be stored in us, as if we're some sort of spiritual battery. God wants to release His power through us to impact the lives of others" (Schmidt 2006, 44). Had Moses simply lived out his quiet life in Midian, he would have failed to release the power God had been placing in him for his entire life. This is what Moses was struggling to see. God had been preparing him all along for this very moment. As we noted earlier, Robert Clinton puts it this way: "In the long haul, God is preparing you for convergence. He is conforming you to the image of Christ (Romans 8:28-29), and He is giving you training and experience so that your gifts may be discovered" (Clinton 1988, 33). God is developing you into the strong spiritual leader he had planned for you from before you were born. Like Moses, we struggle to see.

Throughout my youth, I did not see myself as a leader. I was small, fairly weak, a choir kid, not popular, and not called on to lead anywhere. So I developed a view of myself that was really quite weak. Slowly the Holy Spirit started changing all of that in me. When I first started college, I studied music education and planned to be a choir teacher at the high school level. After two years, I came to realize that although I loved the music classes, I was going to despise getting up early every morning to face a room filled with students that didn't want to be there. So I changed my major. I decided to study business management. Again, although I loved most of the classes, I never even began to grasp business calculus. That wasn't going to work either. So after our junior year of college, Tina and I got married and relocated to South Carolina where she wanted to study youth and music ministry at Southern Wesleyan University (SWU). I planned to enter the business school at Clemson, which was just 4 miles away from SWU. They took one look at my business calculus grade and denied me entry. God and I had a long talk after that rejection, and I finally gave in to what He had been saying to me for a while already. I entered SWU as a Christian ministry student and prepared to become a pastor.

I wondered for years what was with the indecisive pathway I took to ministry. Then it dawned on me what God had done. I grew up feeling weak and powerless. I was now called to minister to people who feel spiritually weak and powerless. I studied music. My first two jobs in ministry required that I lead the choir and often lead worship. To this day, the ability to understand music and its proper use is imperative. I studied business management. Every church I have served required that I generate and manage budgets and spending plans, manage cash flow, look at demographic and market trends around the church, and position the congregation for maximum effectiveness. Oh, and the ministry courses were helpful too! All those changes. All those majors. All those challenges. All those moments the Holy Spirit was using to build into me what He knew I would need.

And He is doing the same with you.

Then, when the time is right, God will call you to a task that is too much. He will have prepared you to do great things on your own. More importantly, He will have prepared you to hear His voice. "God will draw you into a deeper and closer walk with Him so you can trust Him and have faith in Him. He will reveal His purposes to you so you can become involved in His work rather than merely pursuing your own goals and dreams" (Blackaby et al. 2008, 57). So when God shows up in your burning bush experience, argue with Him if you must, but always remember that He designed you, planned for you, guided you, and prepared you for this moment. Yes, the task is too big for you. No, you cannot do this. But God can. There is nothing quite as humbling as seeing God do what only He can do and do it through you.

GREAT LEADERSHIP REQUIRES GREAT RISK

> *Then Moses went back to Jethro his father-in-law and said to him, "Let me return to my own people in Egypt to see if any of them are still alive." Jethro said, "Go, and I wish you well." Now the LORD had said to Moses in Midian, "Go back to Egypt, for all those who wanted to kill you are dead."*
>
> *—Exodus 4:18-19*

Like all leaders, Moses possesses the rod, and all he has to do is believe that he has the power, the ability, to lead. Once he does, he has to wield that power effectively; he has to be willing to act.

—Norman J. Cohen
Moses and the Journey to Leadership

Some years ago, Tina and I were traveling to speak at a missionary retreat in Taiwan. Since we were in Asia, we decided to add about a week to the trip and fly to South Korea, where Tina was born. Her Korean mother and American father had met while he was serving in the military and stationed in South Korea. They were married there, and Tina was born there. Her father came back to the U.S. after his time in the military was over, and he set up a house for the young family.

Some months later, Tina and her mom flew to the U.S. to join her father. None of them ever went back to Korea. In the late 1990s, Tina's mom contracted breast cancer. When the cancer returned for the second time, we pleaded with her to let us take her back to visit South Korea. "No, this is my home now." That's all she would say about it. Sadly, she passed away shortly after that. So when Tina and I had the chance to go to South Korea, we were thrilled.

We made plans to stay with a missionary couple in Seoul. Upon our arrival, they picked us up at the airport. When we arrived at their apartment, he sat us down and described to us where the subway stops were, a few shops, and some areas of the city he thought we should see. Then he let us know what time he would be leaving for work the next day. Well, that wasn't what we expected to have happen. We had traveled with missionaries before, and they normally just took a few days to take us around and show us the town. We most often have our own private guided tours of foreign places. It's really nice. But this guy wasn't going to do that. We were on our own. As we sat in our room, a little disappointed and not really sure what to do, I said to Tina: "We may never get back here. So, let's not sit here in this apartment afraid. Let's go see as much of this place as we can." And she agreed. We did not know the language and had no preset goals. All we did know was that her mother's hometown was a place called Daegu. So I got on the computer and booked train tickets and a hotel. I just made the assumption that we could find people who understood enough

English to help us along the way. The next day, we got on the train and headed to Daegu. Once on the train, we realized there was a dining car. So we went there and ordered kimchee soup. As we sat at that table, we watched out the window as South Korea passed by. We had always wondered why Tina's mom loved the mountains of North Carolina so much, and now we knew. It was beautiful. Then the soup arrived. From that moment on, the trip was borderline magical. The hotel was great. There was even a lady working at the hotel who spoke English! The market was amazing and the people were kind. The trip was one of our favorite experiences. And it never would have happened had we given in to fear. Traveling through a country you don't know and trying to communicate in a language you don't know is risky. However, sitting in an apartment in Seoul wasn't an option either.

Now I realize that the kind of risk Moses is about to take with his life is far more daunting than our little jaunt through South Korea, but the point is the same. Magical moments are only found on the other side of risky decisions. While risk must be considered and calculated, it should not be uniformly avoided. Quoted in the book, *Built to Last*, Theodore Roosevelt said it well, "Far better to dare mighty things, to win glorious triumphs, even though checkered by failure, than to take rank with those poor spirits who neither enjoy much nor suffer much, because they live in the gray twilight that knows not victory, nor defeat" (Collins and Porras 2002, 91). That "gray twilight" is where far too many Christian leaders live. They are too afraid of hurting someone to lead someone. Too afraid of failure to leave whatever is working here, they miss out on God's best. Every great beginning follows a sad ending. Moses left Egypt in a hurry, and it was sad. When he arrived in Midian, he found a place, a family, and a career. Now it's time to leave Midian, and what lies ahead of him seems uncertain. No doubt the work ahead of him is daunting. No doubt what he is about to do is risky. No doubt he is completely incapable. There is also no doubt that this was God's command. Since God called, he will pack up his family and all he has and journey back to Egypt.

Faith is risky.

But God is good.

And when God calls you to risk, always take Him up on it!

3

LEARNING TO GIVE DIRECTION

> *So Moses took his wife and sons, put them on a donkey and started back to Egypt. And he took the staff of God in his hand.*
>
> —*Exodus 4:20*

The task of Christian ministry is so much greater than building an organization or developing a great following. Our challenge, and privilege, is to be workers together with the Spirit in the process of developing mature disciples of Jesus Christ.

—Bruce L. Petersen, Edward A. Thomas, Bob Whitesel
Foundations of Church Administration

In the course of a leader's development, there comes a moment when that leader must begin to actually lead. Up to this point, all of the leadership development we have seen has been internal. God begins our development from the inside and then moves those developed skills, wisdom, and insight outwardly in order to accomplish His goals through our lives. So far, we have been considering that inward development. Now Moses must practice the art of giving direction.

Author Jim Collins begins his book *Good to Great* with this insight:

> Good is the enemy of great. And that is one of the key reasons why we have so little that becomes great. We don't have great schools, principally because we have good schools. We don't have great government, principally because we have good government. Few people attain great lives, in large part because it is just so easy to settle for a good life. (Collins 2001, 1)

The application here is simple — Moses had a good life in Midian. He had a home, family, and meaningful work; it was a really good life. However, God was calling him to greatness.

Far too many people do simply "settle for a good life." They get really comfortable in Midian and just stay there. They have discovered who they are (learn to be). They have discovered how to be a friend and have friends (learn to be a friend). They have even built up enough wisdom to give good advice when that is needed and to help people live better lives (learn to make a difference). And so they settle. No more progress, no more influence, no more … growth. That isn't what God has called us to as leaders. He did not do all of that developmental work in us just to have us settle, especially within the church. The church is the hope of the world. While that phrase seems distant and is easy to utter when we are talking about the universal church, its actual meaning is local. If the church is the hope of the world, then the people in our church are the hope of the world! The building you meet in certainly can't be the hope of the world. I have seen a lot of church buildings in my life and if that's where our hope is then we are in trouble! No, our people are the hope of the world. As God leads us to lead them, they will in turn lead others and one by one the world changes.

> Leading others is like the great sculptor's task. It is the passionate recognition that God's missional future for the church is present among the people of God. The birth stories of Jesus, the annunciation of Mary, and other scriptural narratives tell us that God's future is among the least expected people—even those in the church we write off as unimportant. The leader's role is to help form a people among whom God's future is called forth. (Roxburgh and Romanuk 2006, 146)

That kind of work is not just good work, that's great work!

We must get out of our comfort zone and start giving direction.

GREAT VISION COMES FROM AN INDIVIDUAL, GREAT ACCOMPLISHMENT COMES FROM A TEAM

> *The LORD said to Aaron, "Go into the wilderness to meet Moses." So he met Moses at the mountain of God and kissed him. Then Moses told Aaron everything the LORD had sent him to say, and also about all the signs he had commanded him to perform.*
>
> *—Exodus 4:27-28*

Leaders have to take this one step further. Not only do they have to be willing to test bold ideas and take calculated risks, but they also have to get others to join them on these adventures in uncertainty. It's one thing to set off alone into the unknown; it's entirely another to get others to follow you. The difference between an exemplary leader and an individual risk-taker is that leaders are able to create the conditions where people *want* to join with them in the struggle.

—James M. Kouzes and Barry Z. Posner
The Leadership Challenge

There is one absolute in effective leadership. You cannot do this alone. When God gives a vision to a leader, that leader must then find others who will come alongside him to accomplish that vision. In Moses' case, that partner in leadership will be Aaron. God calls Aaron to help Moses as a concession while Moses is trying to convince God that he has chosen the wrong person. "God, though angered by Moses's response, makes the ultimate concession to his reticent leader: There is another who will serve as his spokesperson; one who is a skilled speaker (4:14-16). Aaron, Moses's older brother, is willing to play second fiddle to Moses, accepting his role as Moses's mouthpiece" (Cohen 2007, 26-27). Every leader needs an Aaron. They need someone who will come alongside and help lead. Cohen continues, "Leaders cannot succeed on their own. The most effective leaders partner with capable individuals whose skills and knowledge complement their own, individuals who are comfortable playing second fiddle" (Cohen 2007, 27).

Over the years that I have been in ministry, God has sent some of the greatest people in the world to walk alongside me. I will forever be grateful for their investment in the vision I believe God has given us for our church and for a movement. It is their skill and insight that have kept everything running and has kept me out of trouble! With that said, there are some requirements for a leader to find and keep people like this around. As a leader, you have to be willing to let others be in charge. You are in charge of the vision, but that does not mean you need to be in charge of anything else. Find great people and let them do great things. Give supervision and insight when necessary, but mostly just find good people and empower them.

But be most careful about the ones who are closest to you.

As the pastor of a large, multi-site church that also engages in church planting, the leadership of our network is a truly complex and daunting task. As we were beginning to plant churches, I became aware that I needed to hire an Executive Pastor. Now this was no easy undertaking. I knew what the job would require, so there were a limited number of people who could work like that. I also knew how I would relate with this person. I was going to hand them the keys to everything. I had already begun to limit my role in day-to-day management, and I needed this person to do that work. That meant that my level of trust for this person had to be off the charts. I recruited and looked for five years. I offered the job to only three people in those five years. Two turned me down, but the one I started recruiting first ultimately said yes. Chris Wagnon served alongside me in this role for seven years, and I never once worried.

Chris was not a pastor. Well, let me say that differently. Chris had no pastoral training. He had spent a career working in government, and this church job was a second career for him. He was actually an awesome pastor. What he did have was intelligence, loyalty, trustworthiness, and a work ethic that would put anyone else to shame! And I did what I knew I was going to do. I handed him the keys to everything. He ran the church. He held the meetings. Along with our Executive Director of Administration, Gayle Bryan, they took care of everything. And I trusted them. So the team worked. That level of trust and balance ultimately is what we must accomplish. An effective and focused team will take a challenging vision and make it a beautiful reality. In the book, *The Advantage*, the author says, "The first step a leadership team has to take if it wants the organization it leads to be healthy—and to achieve the advantages that go with it—is to make itself cohesive. There's just no way around it. If an organization is led by a team that is not behaviorally unified, there is no chance that it will become healthy" (Lencioni 2012, 19). Our team was "behaviorally unified." To say it another way, we were consistently on the same page.

Now, there are two sides to this coin. While I have been clear that the leader or visionary (the Moses in this story) must trust, empower, and release his team of leaders (give them all the keys), the leaders under the visionary must understand their role as well.

> The number-two person is the most important hire, and must be someone who balances the leader's strengths and temperament, shows loyalty without being a sycophant, and has a talent for working well with a variety of individuals and groups. Leaders often find it difficult to share power. Subordinates, meanwhile, may grouse that, given their successes, they should be the ones who receive the ultimate recognition. For the greater good, they should be encouraged to act like Aaron, who revels in his relationship with his younger sibling, even though Moses plays a superior role (4:14-16). (Cohen 2007, 27)

People who support visionaries and leaders are no less important than the visionary leaders themselves. They must be comfortable with the second chair role. Recently, Chris Wagnon decided to retire, again. The Holy Spirit knew that I didn't have another five years to shop for his replacement! So God sent a phone call from one of the leaders I most respect. At the time, Dr. Wayne Schmidt was serving as the President of Wesley Seminary at Indiana Wesleyan University. He called and said, "Mike, you need to talk to this Tim Kirkpatrick. He is looking to be an Executive Pastor, and I think you guys will work well together." So we scheduled him for an interview. Tim is a brilliant young leader and capable of leading at the highest levels, but he feels called to second chair leadership. I immediately reached a level of comfort with him and sensed in my spirit that I could trust him. Now we are building a new team, and we are building a younger team. I jokingly say that we are slowly turning the church over to the 12-year olds. But that, too, is important. Chris and I led the church in a grumpy old man type of fashion. Tim brings an entirely new dynamic. I say all of that to encourage you to keep building teams. God is not going to stop giving you vision, so you can't stop building teams. When one retires or moves away, you must do the work of rebuilding. It's not easy work, but it is important work.

No one accomplishes great things alone. Go find your Aaron or your Moses and get to Egypt. God has some really big things in mind that you are going to want to see happen!

OUR GOAL IS SPIRITUAL, BUT OUR PROCESS IS POLITICAL

> *Moses and Aaron brought together all the elders of the Israelites, and Aaron told them everything the LORD had said to Moses. He also performed the signs before the people, and they believed. And when they heard that the LORD was concerned about them and had seen their misery, they bowed down and worshiped.*
>
> *—Exodus 4:29-31*

Moses and Aaron did not wait for the people to indicate their disbelief prior to performing the signs, as God had instructed; they executed them immediately. The subtle changes ensured that there would be little chance for disbelief or discussion, and that God's promise that the people would heed his voice (3:18) would be fulfilled quickly.

—Zvi Grumet, *Moses and the Path to Leadership*

Our goal is spiritual, but our process is political. People really don't like that phrase, but I still use it. It reminds us of the people side of what we do. No leader can simply walk in front of a crowd and declare that God told him what they should do and expect the crowd to follow. No, that crowd is going to dismiss him as a lunatic! The leader must first get buy-in, build relationship, explain the vision, and paint a beautiful picture of what the future can look like. Then, perhaps the leader can get folks to follow. It takes time, but it won't work any other way. Let's consider both sides of this odd sounding adage.

Our goal is spiritual. If we forget the spiritual goal, we will accomplish nothing of value.

"The ultimate goal of spiritual leadership is not to achieve numerical results alone, or to do things with perfection, or even to grow for the sake of growth. It is to take their people from where they are to where God wants them to be. God's primary concern for all people is not results, but relationship." (Blackaby 2001, 127)

What we are doing as Christian leaders is inviting people into a relationship with Jesus Christ that will alter the trajectory of their lives. That's really heavy stuff. Far too often, we fall into the convenient trap of just counting numbers. Attendance and giving become the only scales we use when assessing progress and success, and this is a mistake. Now, don't get me wrong, the numbers matter. A church that is not growing is declining, and a church that can't pay the bills will not be in ministry long. So I am not suggesting that these numerical measurements are unimportant or should not be followed closely. I also am not suggesting we fall into the other convenient trap of declaring spiritual growth and faithfulness as a sort of replacement for reaching the lost and paying the bills. I simply want to be careful that we keep first things first.

In the office this week, Pastor Aaron Rummage, our Pastoral Care Pastor, interrupted my strict focus on some mundane yet important paperwork. He walked into the room and apologized for the interruption. He had with him a teenage girl from our youth group. He said to me, "Pastor Mike, you don't always get the opportunity to hear these great stories, but I get to hear them all the time. I want you to hear this young lady's story." As the Pastoral Care Pastor at our broadcast campus, Pastor Aaron does much of the follow-up with those who have committed their lives to Christ. He also teaches the baptism class that we take folks through before they get baptized. Hannah was planning to be baptized that next week and needed to take the class ahead of schedule. So this teenage girl took an hour of her day, drove to the church, and sat through a one-on-one class with Pastor Aaron. For the next few minutes, I sat and listened as she told me, through tears, how another young leader in our youth program had brought her to our youth group. She told me about how the Youth Pastor preached a sermon that reached her heart and inspired her to give her life to Christ. That same Youth Pastor grew up in our youth group before going into ministry himself. Now this girl wants to devote her life to serving Christ from here forward. I had the honor of praying with her right there in the office. God is so good!

This is what we are doing here.

I mentioned in an earlier chapter that our leadership team is changing and that I sometimes quip that we are putting the 12 year olds in charge. Actually it's a beautiful thing to watch. Our Campus Pastors at 5 of our campuses came from within the church and two of them grew up at the church. Our Youth Pastor, Children's Pastor, almost our entire worship and creative team and most of our Interns, Residents, and Apprentices all came out of our youth group. The Holy Spirit is changing lives on a daily basis and developing leaders around us, honestly, almost in spite of us.

This is what we are doing here.

As the Holy Spirit leads us to lead, He draws others to lead with us. Whether the story is a wonderful salvation story of a young person or a middle-aged person who chooses to give their life to the work of ministry, the result is nothing short of miraculous.

Our goal is spiritual, and when the Holy Spirit is released to do His work among us, the miracles never cease.

Our goal is spiritual, and that means we will accomplish much of great value!

Our process is political. If we forget the political process, we will accomplish nothing at all.

"As ministry leaders, we're not inviting people to a movie. We're inviting them to join a team of people committed to leading meaningful ministry. We're inviting them to become part of a cause, a vision, something big that changes people's lives. We are inviting them to partner with us in advancing the kingdom. The stakes are very high." (Reiland 2011, 89)

Now, even though our goal is spiritual and that is what we desire to celebrate, it does not negate the fact that our process is political. Watch what Moses and Aaron do first. They *"brought together all the elders of the Israelites."* They understood that if they were going to get buy-in to this huge, unthinkable goal of leaving Egypt, they had to have the right people on the journey with them. Leaders, who attempt to lead without winning over other effective leaders, really don't lead at all. They are simply caretakers of the status quo.

A leader who is not leading leaders is really only holding space. We work with many churches that have long since lost their effectiveness. They have languished, sometimes for generations, with few to no salvations and almost no impact on their local communities. In fact, we often enter communities where people don't even realize the church is there or still active. That is sad. The approach we must take to turn those churches around is extreme. Honestly, these churches lost their effectiveness almost exclusively for one reason. For generations, caretakers instead of world-changers led these churches. They were leaders who did not lead leaders. When that culture takes hold, leaders who do happen into the door can smell the stench of death all over the place. It's not that these leaders don't want to stay and help. The simple fact is they can't stand the culture of dying that has taken over, and they are forced out so that they can find life.

Now, someone may be getting angry with me right now and think that I am devaluing churches that are small and not growing. I am not. There is great value anytime the gospel of Christ is preached. The honor of shepherding any number of people throughout this life and into the next is a great honor for which any human could have ever hoped. However, that isn't the culture to which I've been called. Far too often, I find that this culture is counterproductive to the growth of the Kingdom, and yet it persists. Every generation has those caught in the past or caught in self-centered congregations. A pastor who is an effective caretaker will find plenty of employment opportunity and meaningful ministry, if he can love and care for these folks. Furthermore, for those who are just interested in huddling together and protecting one another from the world, there is also plenty of opportunity. These congregations are really not interested in engaging and reaching the world around them. They are interested in not being tainted by the world around them so they cloister themselves away in their small group of faithful believers. These types have been around since the inception of the church. The Bible shows little animosity toward this group, and there seems to be a meaningful place for them within the Body of Christ. Again, I am not called to this kind of ministry.

In the end, we must be honest about what we are.

If you are looking to maintain and incrementally improve the state of comfort for the slaves in Egypt, that is good work and it is of God.

If you want to set them free, you need a whole different set of leaders and an entirely new way of seeing the future. And you must convince them to buy-in.

You cannot do big things with little teams.

You cannot win great spiritual victories without first winning pressing political battles.

Our goal is spiritual ... but our process is political.

WE ARE NOT BUILDING A CHURCH ...
WE ARE BUILDING A MOVEMENT!

> *The LORD said, "I have indeed seen the misery of my people in Egypt. I have heard them crying out because of their slave drivers, and I am concerned about their suffering. So I have come down to rescue them from the hand of the Egyptians and to bring them up out of that land into a good and spacious land flowing with milk and honey."*
>
> *—Exodus 3:7-8*

Proverbs 29:18, although widely used, is also widely misapplied. The popular translation is, "Where there is no vision, the people perish." (KJV). A more accurate translation of the Hebrew is: "Where there is no revelation, the people cast off restraint." (NIV). There is a significant difference between revelation and vision. Vision is something people produce; revelation is something people receive. Leaders can dream up a vision, but they cannot discover God's will. God must reveal it.

—Henry and Richard Blackaby, *Spiritual Leadership*

I want to revisit this text from Exodus, chapter 3. When you thoughtfully consider what God is calling Moses to do here, it is truly stunning. One would have expected Moses to return to Egypt seeking improvement for the Hebrew people. Perhaps he would have advocated for laws that protected them from beatings. Perhaps he would have slowly implemented laws for slaves to become free and ultimately integrate into Egyptian society. God wasn't interested in any of that, and honestly, he never is. God is not looking for us to simply make people's lives or a nation's laws better. We should strive to do these things, but it is not our mission. God is not looking for us to integrate into the ways and thinking of this world. He is looking to set us apart and lead us to another, better, "good and spacious" land He planned for us long ago. God is not calling Moses to make their lives better; He is calling Moses to lead them out. The goal here will not be an effective organization within Egyptian culture. The goal here is a movement. A nation is to move out of a nation and establish a new nation. Now that's an audacious goal.

As a teenager in a local church youth group, I was intrigued by the notion that the entire world could be reached with the gospel of Christ. It just didn't seem that difficult to me. One person tells another person about Christ. Then that person tells someone else about Christ. All the while, the original person is telling someone else about Christ, who is going to tell someone else about Christ. Before long, everyone is talking about Christ! The math on this is exponential and simple.

But it just didn't seem to work that way.

In college while studying for ministry, movements intrigued me. The Wesleyan revival in England, the First and

Second Great Awakenings here in the U.S., and the more recent advent of a movement I was hearing about that has since become the Calvary Chapel phenomenon. These movements seemed to be experiencing the supernatural, exponential growth I had always believed was possible. The more I read and the more I worked with existing congregations in my early years of ministry, the more I longed for something more. More than just another church, I longed for a movement.

So when we arrived in Southern Maryland in 1999 to pastor New Life Wesleyan Church, Tina and I made it clear to them that we were not interested in just doing the normal church thing. We intended to grow New Life into "the largest church in Southern Maryland." This was a pretty audacious goal for a young pastor and his congregation of less than 100 people. Furthermore, this was no new church plant. New Life had existed for more than 30 years and had never seen significant growth. As I began my work, a local pastor came to me and declared, "There has never been a significant revival in Southern Maryland." I replied: "Well, I guess it's about time then." And we set off on a journey that has been nothing short of miraculous.

As I began looking for words that could communicate what I truly felt the Holy Spirit had revealed to me as His call for our church, I found that the traditional ways of saying things were inadequate. Yes, we wanted to see church growth, but we wanted more. Yes, we wanted to see evangelism, but we wanted more. Yes, we wanted to see increased levels of holy living among our people (discipleship), but we wanted more. And so the Holy Spirit guided me to this movement language, and we adopted this key phrase: We are not building a church; we are building a movement.

Movement implies something that is greater than just an evangelistic outburst or a massive church expansion. It implies, well, movement. Dynamic, uncontrolled, unruly, ill-defined energy, but it also implies deep cultural change. Movements change culture, but not by passing law that can be arbitrary and eventually erased by a different set of rulers. Movements change culture by changing hearts. That is what I wanted to see: a movement. I didn't care if it fit into anyone's definition of what was good or best in church practice. We would use everything we could find to be better, stronger, faster, deeper, holier, and more connected. We would combine those in ways that would be able to reach variant groups and personalities. We would not try to establish a huge church or new denomination; we would trust God to send the Holy Spirit and give us what we could not manufacture — a movement. Consider the following from the book, *Movements That Change The World*:

> Christianity is a movement of movements—monasticism, evangelicalism and Pentecostalism, to name a few. These movements can find expression in movement organizations such as mission agencies and denominations. Movements are one of the key means by which God brings renewal and expansion to the church in its mission. Each new movement has a unique contribution to make to the kingdom—its

"founding charism" or gift of grace. Monasticism modeled a deep devotion to Christ in the face of growing nominalism in the church. The Franciscans' gift to the church and the world was God's heart for the poor. The Reformation upheld the authority of Scripture and restored the truth of salvation by grace through faith. The Anabaptists emphasized the importance of discipleship and the believers' church. The Moravians were an inspiration as the first Protestant missionary order. The Methodists and Salvation Army combined evangelistic zeal and holiness with a heart for the poor. The Pentecostals rediscovered the untamed power of the Holy Spirit. Where would we be today without the influence of these movements? What would we be left with today if their contributions were erased from history? They all had their shortcomings, yet God was at work through them, renewing his church in faithfulness to Christ and his cause. (Addison 2011, 33)

That is what I longed for — a movement of renewal that would change the world, or at least the little world around me. We would build a church, but that would not be the end goal. Once we built the church to strength, we would plant another church that could build to strength. This would be a church that would be different from the mother church. Once that was done, we would plant another one. We would not plant them in some far off city by sending a leader and some dollars; we would plant them across town and across the parking lot. We would take a leader and put him or her on the platform with me and encourage people to go with them. We would intentionally split the church so that healthy groups with healthy leaders and healthy expectations could be launched out. These new churches would be able to build off of the reputation and gravitas of New Life and ultimately be able to reach people that New Life could not reach. Then they would begin to plant churches. When the momentum of all of this grew, New Life would lose control. Pastor Mike would be forgotten. The founding congregation would just be another church. But Christ would be preached all around.

It has been 18 years now and we have planted six churches and started four video venues. All total more than 5,000 people who attend one of our churches each week. Only about 2,800 of those listen to me. As the movement gains ground, I will become increasingly insignificant. That's the plan. As the movement grows, New Life Network will one day dissolve and each of our congregations will simply fold into the Wesleyan Church, our denomination. That's the plan. The network is built to grow but not persist. If we insist on the founding congregation maintaining control, we will choke the movement. If we insist on the founding pastor being in control, we will choke the movement. I guess John the Baptist had it right: *"He must become greater; I must become less"* (John 3:30).

As of this writing, none of our church plants have planted churches, but they are all discussing it. We are not done. We will continue to do this as long as God gives us opportunity and strength. When the opportunity and strength are gone, we will trust the Holy Spirit to take what we have started and do with it what only He can do. We plod on. We have faith. We work. But we understand our goal.

We are not building a church. We are building a Movement!

SPEAK GOD'S WORDS WITH AUTHORITY AND STRENGTH

> *Afterward Moses and Aaron went to Pharaoh and said, "This is what the LORD, the God of Israel, says: 'Let my people go, so that they may hold a festival to me in the wilderness.'"*
>
> —*Exodus 5:1*

God had asked Moses to speak with Pharaoh in a language Pharaoh would understand. In Pharaoh's world, gods don't spontaneously appear to individuals nor are people their primary concern. Chance encounters with divine beings by non-priests are terrifying, and relate to some need that the gods have rather than their genuine caring for people. Thus, while God instructs Moses to tell the Israelites about their impending redemption in fulfillment of the ancestral covenant, He commands Moses to tell Pharaoh about his terrifying, happenstance encounter with the deity and the deity's demand for offerings in the wilderness.

—Zvi Grumet, *Moses and the Path to Leadership*

When God gives you words to say to the people you lead, don't soft peddle them. As I have already pointed out, I was not much of a leader in my younger days. I just didn't think

I had any authority or any real value to bring, so I rarely, if ever, tried to take an authoritative stance. The few times I did ended pretty badly. However, I did understand that the Bible is God's Word. His Word is truth and His Word is authoritative. So when I became a pastor and began delivering sermons on a weekly basis, I preached the Word of God with authority. I didn't ever want to be guilty of soft peddling God's truth.

Unfortunately, this soft peddling of God's holy truth is far too common. Sometimes the truth gets softened out of a desire not to offend or fear of losing a job or position of leadership. No matter why the truth of God's Word is softened, it's wrong. It is not our place to decide that certain parts of Scripture are too outdated or too harsh for modern consumption. It is not our place to weaken the view of God's Word and its authority simply to protect ourselves, or some idea of unity we are striving to achieve within our churches or communities. It is our job to declare the Word of God with power. In this case, the exertion of that power is appropriate, and to fail to exert that power would be inappropriate. "We often think of the poor stewardship of power in terms of individuals who abuse power by exercising it inappropriately or too frequently. The failure to exercise God-given power when necessary is equally poor stewardship" (Schmidt 2006, 163). When we fail to preach God's Word with power, we rob our people of the authority and security that comes from knowing God is always right, always relevant, and always in charge.

Now, having said all of that, we must steward the Word of God and the vision God has given us carefully. There is no room here for cowardice, but there is no room for arrogance either. We must balance how we speak the Word of the Lord, whether it is Scripture preached in a sermon or vision spoken to a group.

Speak Boldly

I honestly think that the biggest transgression in this area in today's church is the weakening of the Word of God in an attempt to placate the society around us. Our enemy, Satan, has brilliantly redefined words like "justice," "sin," "holiness," and "grace." In today's cultural usage of these words, their meaning is nothing even close to the original biblical intent. When we fall victim to the cultural norm of softening the words in Scripture in order to somehow keep people happy and unoffended, we empower these novel and unbiblical definitions. The problem has become so deep that we are challenged to even use the word "sin" any longer. In our culture, to call someone sinful is virtually hate speech. However, sin in the Bible is no slander. It is simply a failure to follow the commands of God, and everyone is guilty of it (Romans 3:23)! I could go on and on about this language problem, but the point is that we are falling victim to it. We must not lose the true biblical language of sin that can be forgiven; justice that does not require someone's blood be shed because Jesus already did that; grace that forgives sin, not redefines it to make it OK; and holiness that is not holier than thou, but is a revered deeper walk in which others should strive for and desire. We don't need to soft peddle the words. We need to reclaim them and their proper meaning. Today's culture desperately needs to understand and see real justice, grace, and holiness. They need to be warned of the dangers of real sin that causes real death. Softening the words will never strengthen the truth.

Speak Intelligently

When you speak with authority, to the best of your ability, always speak with intelligence. Now, listen, you may not be the sharpest tool in the shed, but you can still study. When preparing for a sermon, one should clearly understand the weightiness of being the bearer of God's holy Word.

> The Bible remains the center of Christian life. The history of God's engagement with people from Adam through Abraham to Moses and then to Matthew, Paul, John and others is meaningful in the twenty-first century. But it is wise to keep in mind that it is these stories, not doctrine or moral position, that are likely to engage the sort of people who are more attracted to *Chicken Soup for the Soul* and books by Dr. Phil than to the Bible. (Roxburgh and Romanuk 2006, 181)

Study your Bible and know what it is actually saying. Understand the biblical meaning of words that have been stolen and replaced by the enemy of our souls. Then take the biblical narrative of grace, justice, holiness, and forgiveness

106

and apply it to the people God has placed in front of you who desperately need hope; hope that you are privileged to market on a daily basis.

Speak Appropriately

While we must speak boldly and intelligently, we must also speak appropriately. As Grumet points out in the quote at the beginning of this reading, God and Moses understood that the same message would communicate in entirely different ways to the Hebrews and Egyptians. The two groups had wildly different views of the motivations and operations of deities. Therefore, the same truth had to be spoken in different ways to communicate consistent truth. At times, Moses uses this language barrier to accomplish his goals. At other times, he clearly instructs in new ways of understanding God and His Word and goals. Likewise, we should understand our culture and communicate appropriately within it.

When I insist that we speak boldly, I am not advocating that we should be jerks. There is no reason to be unnecessarily offensive. The gospel has enough offense built into it without us being jerks as we communicate it. When I insist that we speak intelligently, I am not suggesting that every sermon must be a word study to delve into the deeper meaning of each Greek or Hebrew word. There is a time when such teaching is appropriate, and there is a time when the simple retelling of a story can beautifully and effectively communicate life-changing biblical truth. Understanding the difference between being a bully with God's Word and being a wimp with God's Word is a matter of finding balance. Trust the Word of God to be truth in all situations, for all people, in all places, and at all times. Understand what God's Word is actually saying so that you can intelligently convey the life-giving gospel of Christ. Study to know the culture you are speaking to, so that you can appropriately convey the grace and mercy of a God who orchestrated all of human history just to achieve a relationship with us.

DON'T BE SHOCKED WHEN THE WORLD ACTS LIKE THE WORLD

Pharaoh said, "Who is the LORD, that I should obey him and let Israel go? I do not know the LORD and I will not let Israel go." Then they said, "The God of the Hebrews has met with us. Now let us take a three-day journey into the wilderness to offer sacrifices to the LORD our God, or he may strike us with plagues or with the sword." But the king of Egypt said, "Moses and Aaron, why are you taking the people away from their labor? Get back to your work!" Then Pharaoh said, "Look, the people of the land are now numerous, and you are stopping them from working." That same day Pharaoh gave this order to the slave drivers and overseers in charge of the people: "You are no longer to supply the people with straw for making bricks; let them go and gather their own straw. But require them to make the same number of bricks as before; don't reduce the quota. They are lazy; that is why they are crying out, 'Let us go and sacrifice to our God.' Make the work harder for the people so that they keep working and pay no attention to lies."

—Exodus 5:2-9

Whether we lead a family or a country, we all encounter hard times. For a leader, these are the times that truly test our abilities, our commitments, our beliefs. They force us to be inventive, to break out of our comfort zone, to discover strengths we didn't know we had.

—Robert L. Dilenschneider, *Moses: CEO*

I am regularly surprised and disappointed when I see the church shocked because the world acted like the world. Why does this continue to surprise us? It's not new. It goes all the way back to the beginning of time. Mankind has been rebellious toward God ever since Adam and Eve ate that crazy fruit. There seems to be no end to how creative people will get with their rebelliousness! But even when they get crazy, we shouldn't be shocked. We should understand. This world acting like the world is exactly what Pharaoh did, and Moses was not surprised. There was no shock on Moses' part when Pharaoh did not agree to the three-day trek into the wilderness to worship. God wasn't surprised either. In fact, this is exactly how God had told Moses it was going to work.

The elders of Israel will listen to you. Then you and the elders are to go to the king of Egypt and say to him, "The LORD, the God of the Hebrews, has met with us. Let us take a three-day journey into the wilderness to offer sacrifices to the LORD our God." But I know that the king of Egypt will not let you go unless a mighty hand compels him. So I will stretch out my hand and strike the

Egyptians with all the wonders that I will perform among them. After that, he will let you go. (Exodus 3:18-20)

If we know that the world is going to act like the world and we should not let that shock or shake us, then how should we respond? I think the best way to handle it is from a passage in the New Testament. The apostle Paul wrote of this reality in his second letter to Timothy:

For the time will come when people will not put up with sound doctrine. Instead, to suit their own desires, they will gather around them a great number of teachers to say what their itching ears want to hear. They will turn their ears away from the truth and turn aside to myths. But you, keep your head in all situations, endure hardship, do the work of an evangelist, discharge all the duties of your ministry. (2 Timothy 4:3-5)

Paul understood that sinners would act in sinful ways. Therefore, there was no element of surprise when the unbelievers simply found new teachers to teach more acceptable doctrines. That's just the world acting like the world. When they don't like the command of God, they simply change the narrative and do their own thing. However, the Christian leader must react differently.

Keep your head in all situations

When we resist the temptation to be shocked by the world's worldly choices, we teach patience to our people that will give them strength for the journey. Think about it; if we panic or react in anger because of a decision made by a government or corporation, we are communicating to our people that the entity coming against us is a threat to the God who is behind us. That is not what we need to communicate in times of crisis. It is true that Pharaoh has just made the lives of the Israelites more difficult. It is true that he did this specifically because of the demand from Moses and Aaron for the people to have a three-day journey into the wilderness. Moses did what God told him to do, and now there seems to be a negative result to his obedient actions. If Moses expresses any emotion about the Pharaoh, he elevates the Pharaoh to the same level as God in the mind of the Hebrew people. This was a grave danger already. Pharaoh wanted the people to see him as a god. If Moses doesn't keep his head in this situation, he may just confirm the lie that Pharaoh is telling!

Endure hardship

Seeing God do miraculous things is never easy for a leader. Like many out there, I have often wished that this whole serving God and doing the right thing process worked more like a Hollywood movie than real life. But it doesn't. The work of helping people change is never done. No pastor has ever gone home and looked at their spouse and said, "Well, got that done. These people are all fixed, saved, and holy. We can quit now!" It just doesn't work that way. In fact, the entire process is one of endurance. There is a reason the Bible talks so much about endurance. What Moses and the Israelites are entering into is an extended period of tough days. It's going to get worse before it gets better. As a leader focused on God, Moses knew the journey would be worth the struggle. Moses knew God would ultimately deliver His people out of Egypt. Although he did not know how long or the exact process God would use, he knew God, and that gave him all the strength he needed. "Everyone faces discouraging circumstances, but the Scriptures provide the vista leaders need to help them maintain or regain a positive attitude" (Blackaby 2001, 171).

Do the work of an evangelist

All the way through difficult times, keep preaching the gospel. In Moses' case, he had to keep talking to the people about the Promised Land. A land that was so much better than what the Israelites were now experiencing. Though he is dealing regularly with this obstinate King of Egypt, Moses must not come to think that this King is the center of his focus. This King was nothing but a roadblock on his journey to what God had promised. If Moses spends all of his time talking about an obstinate King, he has no time to talk about a Promised Land. In today's church, we can get so turned around by culture and politics that we cease to talk about salvation and grace. That is a deadly mistake. Yes, Pharaoh is a problem. Yes, he is a big problem. Yes, he is what the Israelites want to talk about. However, he is not the point. God is. The story, the victory, and the ultimate triumph will belong to God, not this pouty, little king. Talk about Jesus even in difficult times. In the end, nothing else matters.

Discharge all the duties of your ministry

Stay at the work. Just don't quit. God is working it out in places you cannot see. It may seem that He is taking a break, but that's just because you haven't seen His next move. He is working, so should you. When we allow ourselves to become distracted by the voice of the world, we can make the horrible mistake of turning toward that annoying, grating voice and away from the voice of God. Keep your focus on Him and His calling for you. Keep your eyes completely fixed on His call on your life and His capacity in your crisis. Do the work of ministry while the storm rages. Then when the storm is over, you will still have your eyes on Him.

EXPECT FRIENDLY FIRE

The Israelite overseers realized they were in trouble when they were told, "You are not to reduce the number of bricks required of you for each day." When they left Pharaoh, they found Moses and Aaron waiting to meet them, and they said, "May the LORD look on you and judge you! You have made us obnoxious to Pharaoh and his officials and have put a sword in their hand to kill us."

—Exodus 5:19-21

Trust is often missing in senior management teams, although top managers are loath to admit this in public. If the individuals do not need to work together closely, because the work is routine or because the changes are small and can be made slowly, weak trust is not necessarily a problem. With big changes in a fast-moving world, it's a huge problem. How can you create a sensible vision and strategies for the overall group in a team with low trust? People will think of themselves or of their subgroups first and be protective and suspicious. Smart strategy does not emerge from a pond full of politics, parochialism, and guarded communication.

—John P. Kotter and Dan S. Cohen
The Heart of Change

Moses is facing a crisis of trust. The Israelites don't actually know him. He was raised as an Egyptian Royal and spent the last 40 years as a Midianite shepherd. Now, in rolls this guy from Midian who wants to convince Pharaoh to let his God's people go. There is a real disconnect between what God has Moses trying to do and what the people actually want to see done. They just want to live their lives. Honestly, after all these centuries, they are Egyptians. Their culture has been developed under Egyptian rule, their protection comes from Egyptian soldiers, and their livelihood comes from Egyptian projects. They didn't ask to be delivered, and now their work is harder because of this Midianite shepherd who has a questionable past! Take a look at this from the book, *Moses and the Journey to Leadership*:

> After four hundred years of slavery in Egypt, ensconced in the idolatrous practices of Egypt, the people have assimilated the religious culture of the surrounding society, and it is nearly impossible for them to abandon the known—the familiar religious practices—to worship a God unknown to them. The slaves want to remain slaves, even when the burden of the workload is made more onerous, and the only way they will abandon Egypt and its idols is for God eventually to force them to leave. This is the greatest challenge leaders have to confront: how to maintain hope in the face of their followers' inability to respond to their initiatives and vision. Caught up in their everyday lives or overburdened by responsibility, they cannot even conceive of a better way to live.

Therefore, leaders rarely have instant success. It takes time, patience, and powers of persuasion for a leader to convince his followers to embrace the vision he articulates for the group. Oftentimes, the lack of success has nothing to do with the leader's skills. All leaders must learn to persevere, to overcome personal disappointment, when their efforts to move their community do not produce the hoped-for result. (Cohen 2007, 34)

Like these Israelite slaves caught in the comfort of less than God wants for them, the people we lead are immersed in their own world of confusion, comfort, exhaustion, and familiarity. When we articulate a God-given vision of what life or the church can be, they cannot conceive why we would want to do such a thing. For them, the familiar current reality is what they signed up for; they were born into this. It's all they know. And if it was good enough for my mama, it's good enough for me! The rigidity of the familiar is a devastating wall of resistance for the leader focused on bringing about change. How we react to that resistance is imperative.

Don't lash out

There is literally no need for Moses to be angry with these Israelite slaves. They don't know anything but their slavery. They have no concept of the world that is beyond the boundaries of Egypt, and they know nothing of a Promised Land flowing with milk and honey. All they want to do is make their quota of bricks so they can go home and be with their families. If Moses lashes out in anger at their resistance to his work, he will only alienate them. Anger will validate their worst fears about Moses. In modern ministry, this plays out far too often. A pastor arrives at his new charge and articulates a vision for the future of the congregation. The vision is initially met with worship to God for a new period in the life cycle of the church. Hopes are high and morale is good. Then Pharaoh takes away the straw and the work gets difficult. The changes to the ministries get painful and more difficult. Our favorite senior saint gets their feelings hurt and tears begin to flow. Suddenly, the vision seems too painful and the pathway too dangerous. "How will we make it if so and so leaves?" "I can't stand seeing that person hurt." "What's wrong with the way we have always done it? Why can't we just keep doing what we have always done?" If in this moment, the pastor lashes out in anger, then he displays a lack of compassion that is going to be the final straw.

Don't give up

"So since the pastor can't lash out in anger and the people are not willing to pay such a steep price, then I guess the pastor should just leave." No, not necessarily. Now, understand that there are times when a pastor needs to leave a given congregation. However, once the process of change has begun within the congregation, the pastor really needs to see it through. While there are many who are complaining about the difficulty of the changes, there are others who have their necks out trying to help make the change happen. For the pastor to cut and run now leaves those who have advocated with and for him unprotected and hurt. Now a culture that is truly resistant to change sets in. Trust cannot thrive in such a culture. Therefore, leadership cannot occur. Without leadership, there will be no progress. Without progress, there is only death.

Don't stop trusting God

In my experience, pastors tend to leave just before the tide turns. There is a reason for that. Leadership is toughest just before the tide turns. It feels like you are drowning and no progress is being made, but all of that is part of the process of change. Change is never easy, and change requires God. In Moses' case, God is going to make life in Egypt so unlivable for His people that they will finally be motivated to follow Moses out. "People change what they do less because they are given *analysis* that shifts their *thinking* than because they are *shown* a truth that influences their *feelings*" (Kotter and Cohen 2002, 1).

God is changing their feelings.

For a time, Moses will bear the brunt of the anger brought on by this discomfort. He will battle with the snide comments and jeers of a people who aren't actually motivated to find God's best. In the end, God will win. This is why it is imperative for any leader to continuously talk privately to God, and talk publicly about God, during times of tumultuous change. God is in charge, and He will lead His people to the land He has promised them. He will keep His promises even when that is not our desire. As a leader, we must trust in Him and His ways for our security and future.

"Then the LORD said to Moses, 'Now you will see what I will do to Pharaoh.'" (Exodus 6:1)

IF AT ALL POSSIBLE, LET GOD FIGHT YOUR BATTLES ... HE'S BETTER AT IT!

Then the LORD said to Moses, "Now you will see what I will do to Pharaoh: Because of my mighty hand he will let them go; because of my mighty hand he will drive them out of his country." God also said to Moses, "I am the LORD. I appeared to Abraham, to Isaac and to Jacob as God Almighty, but by my name the LORD I did not make myself fully known to them. I also established my covenant with them to give them the land of Canaan, where they resided as foreigners. Moreover, I have heard the groaning of the Israelites, whom the Egyptians are enslaving, and I have remembered my covenant. Therefore, say to the Israelites: 'I am the LORD, and I will bring you out from under the yoke of the Egyptians. I will free you from being slaves to them, and I will redeem you with an outstretched arm and with mighty acts of judgment. I will take you as my own people, and I will be your God. Then you will know that I am the LORD your God, who brought you out from under the yoke of the Egyptians. And I will bring you to the land I swore with uplifted hand to give to Abraham, to Isaac and to Jacob. I will give it to you as a possession. I am the LORD.'"

—Exodus 6:1-8

To develop a leader to maturity, God enlarges the leader's perspectives of the spiritual dynamics of ministry. The leader must learn to sense the spiritual reality (spiritual warfare) behind physical reality, as well as to depend upon God's power in ministry.

—Dr. J. Robert Clinton, *The Making of a Leader*

Moses will now enter a phase of ministry that can be really frustrating yet supremely satisfying. Through the next chapters, Moses will face complete, obstinate refusal from Pharaoh and continued, though lessening, lack of trust from the Israelites. All of this will happen without him knowing what is coming next, when it is coming, or what will be Pharaoh's response. Moses is about to enter a period of battle, but God is in charge. When he comes out on the other side of this phase, he will be the unquestionable leader of the nation of Israel. However, none of it is because of his doing.

These periods of God's full control can be a bit confusing. As the leader, you will feel as though you should be doing something to move the process forward. However, you have a keen sense that God is telling you not to do anything but wait. For a leader, waiting is painful. There are few things I despise more than waiting. I can get frustrated just waiting in a slow drive-through at a fast-food joint! When the Holy Spirit has you wait, you better settle in for a while. He has work to do and needs you to stay out of the way! During the course of my almost 30 years in ministry, I have faced moments when the Holy Spirit clearly told me to move and move fast. I have faced moments when the Holy Spirit clearly told me to sit and wait. The interesting part is that when I was moving fast, I was gaining less ground in my ultimate leadership goal than when I was sitting and waiting. The difference is really simple. When I am moving fast and working hard, we, as a movement, are accomplishing everything of which we are capable. When I sit down and let the Holy Spirit do the work, we, as a movement, are accomplishing everything of which the Holy Spirit is capable.

Be careful here. The lesson is not to stop trying, to quit working, and to let God do it all. Some seem to think that way but that's not the point. In the moments when the Holy Spirit takes over and has you sit this one out, God is doing what only He can do. Listen again to how this section of Scripture begins: *"The LORD said to Moses, 'Now you will see what I will do to Pharaoh'"* (Exodus 6:1). This is not the time for Moses to decide that he is going to take out Pharaoh. That would have simply been some sort of human-inspired military coup that would have just resulted in another human leader of another human nation. This was going to be different. God was going to teach something very important to Moses, to the Israelites, and to Egypt.

Moses

God was going to teach Moses faith. Moses was hesitant to respond positively when God called him from the burning bush. That was largely due to Moses' own insecurities and perceived weaknesses, but it was, at least in part, a problem with Moses' faith. God has never done what Moses is now declaring God is going to do. In the beginning, it seems plausible that Moses himself was not certain God would actually accomplish this. Again, Grumet implies that Moses was likely trying to sabotage his initial encounter with Pharaoh.

> Thus, just as Moses made subtle adjustments in his approach to the Israelites to ensure the success of his mission to them, he also introduced subtle changes in his mission to Pharaoh to ensure its failure. From Moses's perspective, the net result of the failure of the mission would be God's miraculous intervention to free the people, but that would not require Moses's involvement. As far as Moses is concerned, he has completed his mission and is now free to return to his pastoral life in Midian. (Grumet 2014, 43)

God had so much more in mind for Moses. Now Moses would sit and watch while the *"mighty hand"* of God dealt devastating blows to the unsuspecting Pharaoh.

Israelites

God was going to teach the Israelites a lesson about His faithfulness. "The promise made to the patriarchs will be fulfilled through Moses" (Cohen 2007, 31). God will always uphold His covenants. God Himself had promised Abraham, Isaac, and Jacob that their descendants would one day possess this land where they were living as strangers and aliens. Now, at long last, God was going to keep that promise. Now the family had become a nation. God was ready to birth that nation out of its bondage and in to its glorious promise. The Israelites had never seen God fulfill His promises like this before; in fact, no one had. Now, in this moment, through this man, Moses, God was going to show up and show off! Israel would never forget this lesson!

Egypt

The Egyptians were to learn a lesson as well. They were about to learn about the true God of Heaven. For centuries, they had served their chosen array of gods and demigods. They had defied everything around them in an attempt to understand and control their natural world. They had been holding back the Israelites from worshiping the one true God and expecting their weak substitute gods to protect them. God is about to show them He is boss.

ALWAYS LET GOD FIGHT GODS ... YOU LEAD PEOPLE

The LORD, the God of the Hebrews, has sent me to say to you: Let my people go, so that they may worship me in the wilderness. But until now you have not listened. This is what the LORD says: By this you will know that I am the LORD.

—*Exodus 7:16-17*

The *spiritual warfare* process item refers to those instances in ministry where the leader discerns that ministry conflict is primarily supernatural in its source and essence. He depends of God's power to solve the problem in such a way that his leadership capacity, particularly his spiritual authority, is demonstrated and expanded.

—Dr. J. Robert Clinton, *The Making of a Leader*

From Exodus, chapter 7 all the way through chapter 11, God sends plagues on Egypt. Each plague is destructive to the financial, social, and religious hearts of the Egyptian people. In fact, God specifically targets the Egyptian Gods with these plagues. In the book, *Moses: Faithful Servant of God*, the author highlights this targeted approach by God as He weakens the Pharaoh and strengthens Moses:

What is clear is how these plagues targeted the Egyptian gods. Some plagues challenged particular gods, such as the plague of darkness which was directed against the sun god, Ra. However, that close correlation is missing with some of the other plagues (for example, hail). Nevertheless, the plagues as a whole were a clear signal that Yahweh is more powerful than any and all Egyptian gods. The point is implied in Exodus 12:12 and 15:11 and made explicit by Moses' father-in-law: "Jethro was delighted to hear about all the good things the LORD had done for Israel in rescuing them from the hand of the Egyptians. He said, 'Praise be to the LORD, who rescued you from the hand of the Egyptians and of Pharaoh, and who rescued the people from the hand of the Egyptians. Now I know that the LORD is greater than all other gods, for he did this to those who had treated Israel arrogantly'" (18:9-11). (Lennox 2016, 69)

Christian leaders should keep a few things in mind as they lead the people of God through this fallen world.

Spiritual warfare is real

I don't want anyone jumping off the deep-end on this one, but we have to deal with the realities at hand. While I do not look for or tend to find demons and spirits around every corner, the fact remains that we are in a spiritual war in this Christian life of ours. Throughout my ministry, I have from time to time faced this type of spiritual encounter. I have no desire for it and do not go seeking it. However, when spiritual battle is entered, there is no choice but to face it. Once I was in one of the buildings where one of our congregations is housed. The history of this congregation was extremely divisive. There was a spirit of anger and division that just hung over the place, like a dark cloud. One afternoon, I was alone in the building. My son, Robert, had gone out to get some dinner for us. As I walked around the church, I was suddenly struck by a deep sense that a battle was about to ensue. I began to hear running sounds and rhythmic knocking sounds throughout the building. I must tell you that my initial emotional response was to leave and just run away, but I didn't. Once I stood my ground and continued to pray out loud, the fear passed. Now I was angry. In my mind, I thought, "How dare this thing come in here and defile the house of God." I began to open every exterior door, and as I did so, I prayed out loud, actually yelling at the spirit: "Yeah it's true; I would have run away from you! But I serve a God that does not back down and I am not going to let you win this day! Get out!" I kept walking around the entire building following the sounds wherever they went demanding in the Name of Jesus that they leave. Then it all just stopped. The building was quiet again. I continued to pray over the building until Robert returned. He took one look at me and asked, "What happened?" I told him and we both prayed over the building for a while longer and then left.

You are no match for the enemy

Upon hearing a story like that, some would want to rush out and "kick some devil butt!" Yeah, stand down cowboy. It's not like that. As humans, we need to understand that these spiritual entities are stronger than we are. There is a reason that Moses is nothing more than a messenger during these plagues. God defeats the gods of Egypt, not Moses and not Aaron. In moments when we face spiritual warfare, we must continually understand that we cannot overcome and win in these situations. Only God can win. The power of the Holy Spirit will care for us in these moments and nothing else is sufficient. Don't go looking for spiritual trouble. A man named Sceva is recorded in Acts 19 as having seven sons who went looking for a fight with a demon, and let's just say it didn't end well. You must be fully surrendered to the Holy Spirit and fully trusting in His power in these moments. If you try and do it alone, it will not end well.

The enemy has already been defeated

Now the good news is that the enemies of God have already been defeated. In his letter to the general church, the apostle John gives us these words: *"You, dear children, are from God and have overcome them, because the one who is in you is greater than the one who is in the world"* (1 John 4:4). While it is true that we should not be out looking for a spiritual fight, we should not be afraid when we find ourselves in one. God has already defeated the forces of darkness through the sacrifice and resurrection of Jesus who is the Christ! We can be confident and brave because just like in Moses' day, God will fight for us and He will always win!

WHEN GOD SAYS GO ... BE READY TO GO!

> *This is how you are to eat it [Passover meal]: with you cloak tucked into your belt, your sandals on your feet and your staff in your hand. Eat it in haste; it is the LORD's Passover.*
>
> *—Exodus 12:11*

In successful change efforts, the first step is making sure sufficient people act with sufficient urgency—with on-your-toes behavior that looks for opportunities and problems, that energizes colleagues, that beams a sense of "let's go." Without enough urgency, large-scale change can become an exercise in pushing a gigantic boulder up a very tall mountain.

—John P. Kotter and Dan S. Cohen
The Heart of Change

Suddenly, everything changes.

Over the years that I have served in a leadership capacity, I find that this truth is a constant. Change, even when worked toward or expected, tends to happen rapidly. Now, I don't mean to communicate that it happens instantly. Actually, real, substantive change takes a really long time to see happen.

133

However, when the actual change occurs, it will feel like it happened overnight! "Centuries of delay ended in an instant as the command to go spread among the Israelites from house to house. In haste they collected their belongings, even their unbaked bread, and traveled from Rameses southeast to Sukkoth (Ex. 12:37)" (Lennox 2016, 92). The challenge with this sudden occurrence of change is one of preparation. All too often, we hope for and work toward a change in our lives or in our leadership. When that change occurs suddenly and unexpectedly, we aren't ready for the fallout. We must do the work of being ready for the change and staying ahead of the fallout.

Plan for the change

Every good leader needs to be looking toward what is next for the progress and development of the group or organization that he or she leads. We just have to remember that no organization exists for long in a static pose. Organizations, just like people, are either progressing or regressing. They are either expanding or contracting. These states or change are not as easy as it might seem to define. Progress seems to always be positive. However, there are times when an organization needs to regress back to the core of why they exist. Further progress in the wrong direction is actually more devastating than regression back to the core of meaning. Expansion always seems to be the right answer, but expansion beyond what is sustainable will lead to the destruction of the individual or organization. Sometimes a strict diet is required to get rid of unhealthy expansion. There are times when either is the right call, but which is right, right now? Making this decision requires time, effort, thought, and planning.

> In successful large-scale change, a well-functioning guiding team answers to questions required to produce a clear sense of direction. What change is needed? What is our vision of the new organization? What should not be altered? What is the best way to make the vision a reality? What changes strategies are unacceptably dangerous? Good answers to these questions position an organization to leap into a better future. (Kotter and Cohen 2002, 61)

In short, good change requires good planning.

Communicate the change

When Moses explains to the people that they should *"eat it in haste,"* there had been no call from the Pharaoh. The people had not been set free and no actual change had taken place. Moses' explanation nonetheless had made perfect sense to the Israelites. The reason is communication. Moses had been talking to the Israelites about leaving Egypt since his arrival in chapter 4. We are now in Chapter 12. Moses communicated clearly (and often) the vision of leaving this life of slavery and beginning a new nation that would occupy a land that had been promised by God to their forefathers. He had been communicating this vision for so long that the idea of being prepared for the moment when it came to fruition made sense. "In successful change efforts, the vision and strategies are not locked in a room with the guiding team. The direction of change is widely communicated, and communicated for both understanding and gut-level buy-in. The goal: to get as many people as possible acting to make the vision a reality" (Kotter and Cohen 2002, 83). In our organizations or personal lives, we must establish a vision for what the future can look like and then implement that vision with tenacity and patience. This way when the *"eat it in haste"* moment comes, people are ready or even impatiently excited about the changes that are at hand.

Structure for the change

This idea could be missed if one didn't look closely at the biblical text. Moses has done the work of having all the elders of the people engaged in planning for this moment. God has already warned him that when the moment comes, it will be sudden and they must move instantly. There will be no time for delay. Moses has the people packed up, fed, organized, and ready to go.

> Visions seen only by the leaders are insufficient for generating organized movement. Leaders must get others to see the exciting future possibilities. They breathe life into visions. They communicate hopes and dreams so that others clearly understand and share them as their own. They show others how their

values and interests will be served by the long-term vision of the future. (Kouzes and Posner 2012, 100)

Long before a vision becomes a reality, the effective leader has either changed the structure of the organization or empowered the structure of the organization to support the change that is coming. In Moses' case, there was a leadership structure already in place that the Egyptians had been exploiting for their purposes. The elders of the people had directed the work that was demanded by the Egyptians. Now they would direct those same people to move from being workers to being travelers. The people of Israel completely change their reality and their nation in order to finally become what God always intended them to be. And it all starts in one night!

Ride the change

"During the night Pharaoh summoned Moses and Aaron and said, 'Up! Leave my people, you and the Israelites! Go, worship the LORD as you have requested. Take your flocks and herds, as you have said, and go. And also bless me.'" (Exodus 12:31-32)

The moment they had been waiting for has arrived. More than 400 years of captivity in Egypt is ending in one sweeping moment. As a leader, we must understand a reality that might easily be missed. From the beginning of chapter 4 through the end of chapter 12, Moses and Aaron, along with some group of elders, have worked daily to convince the Pharaoh to let the people go. Their entire focus has been on this one issue.

137

Likewise, Pharaoh has stressed daily over this request from Moses that to him seems irrational and impossible. Plague after plague. Meeting after meeting. Delay after delay. Broken promise after broken promise.

This has taken forever!

That is not how the people experience it. For them, life has not changed. Each day, they are getting up, making breakfast, doing the back-breaking work demanded by the Egyptians, and then sinking back down onto their beds exhausted. Their lives have not changed. They have not been part of the negotiations between Moses and Pharaoh. Most of them have not even been privy to the experiences of their elders or the information they may possess. They have seen the plagues. They know that Moses is working. They may have even experienced the worry and concern on the faces of the Egyptians they encountered. But their lives have not changed.

Until now.

Suddenly, they observe this odd ritual that will now be known as the Passover, there seems to be a massive amount of death among the Egyptians, and the elders burst into their communities and say: "Let's go! Right now!" It has got to be shocking. But because of the information they do have, or perhaps because of the trust they have in their particular elder, they get up and go.

Riding the wave of change once it arrives is the point where many leaders fail. Whether they failed to build the proper structures for the change at hand, or whether they were just personally unprepared for the massive up-swell of change, many leaders are swept under in this moment. The only way to properly ride out large-scale change is to be prepared for it when it comes. Like a surfer in rough seas, we must be prepared for the wave. Those who are prepared and have put in place the right equipment and structure can stand and ride the energy of this creative and/or destructive force. Those who are not prepared will simply find themselves tossed about and taken under. With no real sense of which way is up and suddenly bleeding from the jagged coral underneath, they are now in pain and gasping for air. They plead for it all to slow down and somehow go back to the smooth, easy seas when they were at least treading water. In the pain, panic, and confusion, they fail to realize that the ones who were prepared are riding the very force that is driving them under. Better yet, for those who are prepared, that ride will end on the soft, sandy shores of a paradise that is nothing less than God's Promised Land.

Change is coming.

When it comes, it will be sudden.

Be ready.

REMEMBER GOD'S MATH: FINDING BALANCE BETWEEN FAITH AND PRESUMPTION

> *The Egyptians urged the people to hurry and leave the country. "For otherwise," they said, "we will all die!" So the people took their dough before the yeast was added, and carried it on their shoulders in kneading troughs wrapped in clothing. The Israelites did as Moses instructed and asked the Egyptians for articles of silver and gold and for clothing. The LORD had made the Egyptians favorably disposed toward the people, and they gave them what they asked for; so they plundered the Egyptians.*
>
> *—Exodus 12:33-36*

You must maintain a long-term focus for one simple reason: It's the only way you can be certain you'll capture the profits that investments offer — and avoid taking the full brunt of occasional downturns.

—Ric Edelman, *Rescue Your Money*

It was the fall of 1998 when Tina and I had just traveled to Southern Maryland to consider taking over as the pastor of a struggling church of less than 100 people. Upon arrival, we found a congregation that had not grown significantly during their entire 30-plus-year history. They were debt-ridden having just built a new building without seeing the normal accompanying growth that comes with a building project. They were discouraged. As they interviewed us, they were seriously considering hiring a retired pastor who would just "take care" of them as they weathered this storm of difficulty. Their only other option was Tina and I, but there was a catch. We were not going to come up here without staff-help. So, this small, debt-ridden, discouraged congregation had to make a choice. Pay a retired guy part-time to take care of them, or hire this crazy, young guy and his even younger staff guy. Honestly, the math worked on the first scenario. The retired guy would have done the preaching and visited with the families and held the church together. Furthermore, with only a part-time salary to handle, they would have been able to make the mortgage payments and perhaps survive. The math on the second scenario just didn't work. If they couldn't pay their current bills how were they ever going to handle those bills and two staff salaries. The math just didn't work. But after prayer and discussion, they did the unthinkable; they stepped in to the unworkable. They stepped out in faith and entered into the arena of God's math.

What they did not know at the time was that Pastor Jon Ward and I had decided that we were going to make this work no matter what it took. We had already decided that we would take side jobs and work bi-vocationally if needed in order to accomplish what God had in mind. However, we weren't going to tell them that. The congregation needed to take the risk and trust God for the deliverance. We, as the leaders, needed to be willing to take the risk and sacrifice wherever we were called to do so. When both of those points of surrender had been met, then God could do His math and teach all of us a new level of faith.

This is the moment that the Israelites faced as they grabbed their bags and left Egypt. They were a community of slaves. They had never traveled. They had never owned anything. They were slaves. Now, they were called to leave the only comfort they knew and follow a person they did not know. What they were doing had never been done. The simple logistics of it were unthinkable. Moving that many people from one place to another. Finding water, finding food, finding resources. They couldn't fight their way out of Egypt; they were slaves, not warriors. Even if Pharaoh ever did let them go, they would leave penniless. But God had a plan. Like most of God's plans, the payoff didn't come until the movement started. They still had nothing when the elders rushed about telling the people, "It's time! Let's go!" On the way out, God performed a miracle. As they left Egypt, they began to ask the Egyptians for silver, gold, and clothing. They asked for anything that would help fund their journey as they left, and the Egyptians gave them everything! These slaves were not only going to win their freedom, they were going to impoverish their slave drivers. All of this without the Israelites drawing a single sword or engaging in a single fight. God took nothing and gave them everything!

That's God's math.

Now there are two common threads in the story of Moses and in the story of New Life. I want to consider both of them here, so that we avoid two massive points of failure.

Failure of Faith

The first point of failure is to lack faith. Most often leaders and organizations look into a bleak future and see no hope. They fail to be optimists about what is in front of them, and they instead claim themselves to be realists who are simply going to give in to the current reality of doom and gloom. These folks would have looked at the Israelites in Moses' day and simply concluded that the effective movement of that many disempowered people out of an unwilling empowered nation through an inhospitable desert to an already occupied land, was simply not realistic. Honestly, by all human measurements, they would have been right about that. They would have then begun the process of incremental improvement in the lives of the Hebrew slaves in the hopes that one day, many generations in the future, they would be fully integrated into Egyptian society in such a way as to have a better life. These folks always mean well, but they always miss God's best.

Failure of Reason

Then there are the folks who market in faith alone. These folks look at any situation and see only the positives. They fail to note the challenges that are front and center with the realists.

These optimists are committed to the dream of what is possible with no consideration of the damage and dangers along the way. They can only see the Promised Land. However, they fail to note that between them and the Promised Land is an Egyptian army, poverty, hunger, thirst, a desert, and people who already live in your promised land who are not likely to agree with your claim to ownership. Multiply all of this by a couple million people and you have an idea of the level of blind faith it would have taken for one of these optimists to win the day.

In the end, what we must do is find the balance between faith and presumption. Faith is required if we are ever to see God's greatest and best in our lives. Presumption presumes that God must come through if we simply step out. One should never doubt God's willingness and capacity to do the impossible, the miraculous. By the same token, one should never presume that God must or simply has to provide for us or deliver us. Our work is to be on God's timetable, not demand that He live on ours. In order to properly process this balance between faith and presumption, let me suggest two sides of faith that will help us.

Take the Risk ... Trusting

Let me just say, faith requires risk. There is no way around it. If you are going to see God do the miraculous in your life, it will only be because you have stepped in to an arena where the miraculous is absolutely required. In our lives and in the lives of the organizations we lead, there are moments when you have to finally grab your bags and go! Those moments come suddenly and we never have enough data to absolutely know the outcomes. When following a command from God, we must go, even with lacking or faulty data. The Israelites stepped out in to the unknown without the capacity to accomplish what they were setting out to do. God provided. In this one moment, God not only provided the permission to go but the resource they would need to get where they were going. If you really think it through, when the Israelites finally, years later, build the tabernacle, it would have been Egyptian gold and silver that was donated by the people for the building of the Ark of God and the tabernacle. God, in this one moment, provided materials they could not even conceive of needing. God already had a plan for it, but the Israelites had to go before God gave. They were already packed, already leaving, and on the way out of town when the Egyptians willingly gave to them all the wealth of Egypt. Faith requires risk.

Take the Risk ... Sacrificing

As the leader, risk requires a willingness to sacrifice. The leaders who were at the front of this exodus were sacrificing a great deal to get this done. Moses had already sacrificed his comfortable life in Midian — a level of security and comfort he would never experience again. Aaron and the elders were already living at the very top of the only reality they had ever known. It's not likely that the elders themselves were making the bricks and breaking their backs. They were busy managing the people in order to keep the Egyptians happy and as friendly as possible toward the Hebrew people. Now they were leaving everything that was comfortable to follow God's plan. It wasn't an upgrade for them. This new life was going to be harder and riskier, but they sensed that God was in it and sacrificed what they had in order to find what God had for them.

Now let's go back to the New Life story. Tina and I did move to Southern Maryland, and Jon and Ashley came with us. We arrived in January of 1999 and quietly Jon and I looked around to consider what jobs we might take if that became necessary. But it never did. From the first Sunday we arrived, the Holy Spirit began sending new people and new resources. The income at the church increased. I worked with our creditors and found ways to get current with them and find some temporary relief. The congregation worked and they sacrificed giving above and beyond what was normal for that size group of people. That first year, we needed to see just around $300,000 come in to make our bills. While I don't remember offhand exactly what our total income was after 12 months, I know that we have never missed a payroll or a bill. Jon and I never had to take jobs outside the church, and God continued to bless. We could never have imagined back then the reality that New Life Network of Churches is today. We just knew what God had called us to. The Holy Spirit convinced us at our own burning bush. Like Moses, we looked into the face of the impossible math and just assumed that God's math is not like ours. On that point, we were right!

DON'T FEAR ENDINGS

> *All the Israelites did just what the LORD had commanded Moses and Aaron. And on that very day the LORD brought the Israelites out of Egypt by their divisions.*
>
> —*Exodus 12:50-51*

Leading a missional church is not easy. It is more than a call to commitment. It is more than a call to loyalty or duty. Inviting people to become part of a missional church is inviting them to sacrifice themselves for the cause of Christ without any reciprocal promise that there is something in it for them. Self-will and self-ego are willingly "crucified" for the sake of the mission. However, there is a promise. The promise is that there is a resurrection after the crucifixion.

—Bruce L. Petersen, Edward A. Thomas, Bob Whitesel
Foundations of Church Administration

The Israelites are now on a mission. They are headed toward the Promised Land and they are all in. There really is no turning back at this point. They have seen the destruction of Egypt through the plagues of God and have now plundered the Egyptians as they left. There is no going back. The same can be said of a church when rapid growth takes hold. All of the structures of the church must change. Physical structures must be expanded to accommodate numerical growth. Spiritual structures must expand in order to accelerate spiritual growth. Leadership structures must expand in order to accommodate people, direction, inspiration, and development. Everything must change.

I am sometimes hesitant to tell the story of New Life and the tremendous growth that God has sent our way. I don't want to discourage anyone, and sometimes the stories of someone else's miracle leaves a person feeling discouraged since they have yet to see any of their miracle happen. The real reason for hesitation is different. To be entirely honest, I am not fully convinced that most congregations are willing to pay the price for growth. I am not even certain that most pastors are willing to pay the price. In order for any person or organization to grow, there must be a purging, a dying to some things, and an adding or adherence to other things. This is painful and difficult stuff. Letting go of what we have worked hard to build is no easy task. Oftentimes, the leader or pastor is the one who needs to let go, and just can't. Other times, it's parishioners, followers, or employees who must let go of old practices and structures in order to see progress. Whoever must let go, the process is not easy.

When Tina and I arrived in 1999, we came to know and love a group of around 100 truly faithful and surrendered church people. We were amazed at their willingness to allow us to lead and allow us to change things. I am honestly not entirely sure what caused that surrendered attitude in these people. Perhaps it was the fact that the building they were in was so new, and they had not really established a solid relationship with the place. Perhaps it was the years of meeting in a theater or other space as this new building was being built. Whatever it was, it served us well. They were willing to change anything short of our theology to accomplish our mission. Most of them are still with us now 18 years later. This is what most church people and pastors don't understand. The church that Tina and I arrived at in 1999 no longer exists. There isn't a single wall or floor that hasn't been changed or torn down. The woods behind the church are gone and replaced by a new, larger worship center. The small group camaraderie is gone since the original people now attend service at different times and some are with our church plants in different places. New Life Wesleyan Church circa 1999 had to die in order for New Life Wesleyan Network of Churches circa 2017 to exist. And none of that was easy.

You might think that it must be nice that we have all of that change stuff behind us, but that just isn't true. We must now live in a constant state of change. It seems to me that every time I attempt to allow the systems to settle down and settle in a little, the Holy Spirit slaps us with even more change. It can get a bit frustrating, but it is absolutely necessary. When Pastor Jon Ward and I arrived in Southern Maryland, I remember saying to him, "Our job is to build a structure so strong that the snot-nosed kid who tries to replace us really struggles to take it apart." My heart was right, but the thinking is messed up. I wanted to build a church that was strong and resilient, so that no matter what challenges arose, the church would remain powerful and stable. I never wanted this congregation to face financial struggles or attendance struggles again, even after I was dead and gone. So I set out to build a strong structure. The problem was that any structure strong enough to survive crisis on its own was not flexible enough to allow for continued growth. As God was opening doors for church planting and campus planting all around us, our structure threatened to become stricture. I began to learn a new lesson.

Don't be afraid of endings.

The New Life of 1999 had to die in order for the New Life of 2017 to exist. Now the New Life of 2017 will have to die for the New Life of 2027 to exist. It's a never-ending cycle. In the book, *Built To Last, the authors point to this cycle*: "Comfort is not the objective in a visionary company. Indeed, visionary companies install powerful mechanisms to create *dis*comfort— to obliterate complacency—and thereby stimulate change and improvement *before* the external world demands it" (Collins and Porras 2002, 187). This death to life cycle is never-ending. There will not come a day in our church when I can finally sit back and decide that we have arrived at the perfect balance and now I can just rest. If that day does arrive in my mind, then I must be mature enough to realize that it is time for me to go; I have become the problem and not the leader!

Had the Israelites simply decided to stay, Moses would have not had the privilege of leading them out. Likewise, had Moses simply decided not to die to his old life in Midian, the Israelites would have been forced to wait for God to raise up another leader. Both the leader and the people had to agree to a crucifixion in order to experience a resurrection. I use the harsh language here on purpose. In the words of Dr. Wayne Schmidt in his book, *Surrender,* "There is no power in partial surrender. Surrender must apply not only to all areas of life, but also to all levels of the person: spirit, soul, and senses" (Schmidt 2017, 75). This truth applied to a church demands that surrender must be complete. Every ministry, every staff person, every worship service, every sermon, and every point surrendered to the ultimate goal of reaching every existing and coming generation with the gospel of Christ. This will not be easy. This will be painful. This will be difficult. But this will be worthy of our sacrifice.

Don't be afraid of endings. They lead to beginnings!

4

LEARNING TO BUILD STRUCTURE

> *And on that very day the LORD brought the Israelites out of Egypt by their divisions.*
>
> —*Exodus 12:51*

Just as the skilled pastor should have a basic understanding of counseling and psychology, a rudimentary understanding of organizational behavior should also be seen as indispensable. Those shepherds who are bereft of such skills may need to surround themselves with staff and/ or lay people qualified in these vital disciplines. A foundational understanding of the behaviors and personalities of organizations must be integrated into leadership strategies to ensure their appropriateness and viability.

—Mark Smith and David W. Wright
The Church Leader's MBA

In our journey to finding the heart of a leader, we have been through multiple stages of development.

Learning to Be — This is a crucial starting point for our development. Before we can learn to be what God has for us, we must learn to be in the presence and will of our Creator.

Learning to Make a Difference — We must do the work of learning. Through desert seasons and quiet places, we must develop the wisdom that can come alongside our hearts. Then we can actually make a positive difference in the lives of those we lead.

Learning to Give Direction — Once we find and accept God's ultimate call in our lives, we must do the work of learning to actually implement what God has called us to do.

Now we will consider the work of learning to build structure. Someone asked me recently what the difference was between pastors of small to medium sized churches and leaders of movements. My answer was really quite simple. Structure. The work of building a small to medium sized church is the work of building relationships. If I can be a friend (or at least happily connected) to 50 people and those 50 attend my church with their families, then I should be pastoring a church of around 150 people. The greater my capacity to build and maintain those types of relationships, the larger that type of congregation can grow. If we are ever to break out of that mid-size range, we must do so through structure. Two simple concepts here:

Relational Structure

I have often said that I am a 150 guy. That means that I have the capacity, on my own, to build a church to 150 in attendance. I know this because I have tested the theory. I have actually built a church of 150 and then watched it stall and grow no further. However, during my time at my last assignment in North Carolina, I did the work of understanding structure. When we arrived in Maryland, I had a group of church volunteers that were highly committed and motivated. I gathered them together and asked a favor. "May I treat you like staff and treat our meetings together like staff meetings? You all know I can't pay you, but can I lead you as if I were paying you?" They graciously agreed. As the months passed, they remained true to that promise. We held "staff meetings" on a regular basis, and I began to be able to do the work of ministry through them rather than doing it myself. As the church grew over time, many of them ended up actually being on our paid staff. The lesson I learned from that was invaluable. I may be a 150 guy, but I can accomplish more if I find a way to work through my 150 than if I simply work with my 150. Today, I still consider myself a 150 guy. It's just that now I am able to work through them and multiply the results of our efforts.

Layered Structure

Eventually any organization will outgrow its structure. In other words, though I can do much more by working through my 150 than with my 150, eventually our church will reach the place where it goes beyond the capacity of the 150. What then? The answer is layers. Just like I repeated and multiplied my abilities by working through people rather than just with people, I found that we could build a subsequent layer of leadership. This not only multiplied the leader, but it actually multiplied the team that the leader leads. The best example of this is our church plants or venues. Here, we simply multiply the entire team of leaders in a different location. I may or may not be the communicating pastor, and honestly, that isn't the most pressing issue. We are able to duplicate the entire leadership team from the main campus to another campus. Furthermore, we duplicate the entire volunteer team at another campus. Now there is another layer of leadership developing underneath the layer of leadership that has already been working.

As Moses leaves Egypt with the people, there is an organizational structure in place *"by their divisions."* Like any organization, Moses soon realizes that the old structure is insufficient for the new challenges. Therefore, he must discover a new form of organizational structure. There are many parts to this, and we will be forced to begin with philosophical insights. However, we will ultimately see the beauty and God-given power of a Spirit-filled and God-centered structure.

END GAME THINKING

> *The LORD said to Moses, "Consecrate to me every firstborn male. The first offspring of every womb among the Israelites belongs to me, whether human or animal." Then Moses said to the people, "Commemorate this day, the day you came out of Egypt, out of the land of slavery, because the LORD brought you out of it with a mighty hand."*
>
> —*Exodus 13:1-16*

Once a business class was asked what they considered to be the greatest book on strategy. Several members answered the Bible. They were correct. God initiated his plan in the Garden of Eden in Genesis 2, built a nation to receive the Messiah with numerous prophecies pointing the way, unfolded the plan of salvation in the New Testament, and revealed the final victory at the Holy Book's end. When humankind fell to sin, God had a plan to rescue the race of Adam.

—Bruce L. Petersen, Edward A. Thomas, Bob Whitesel
Foundations of Church Administration

In order to lead effectively, you must envision the end from the beginning. While it is true that circumstances and situations may arise that alter our course, we must begin with some concept of the end. Without this concept of destination, next steps are impossible to define. The leader cannot simply look to the future. There must be a strong tie to the past from the beginning in order to properly arrive at the future.

> As contradictory as it might seem, in aiming for the future you need to look back into your past. Looking backward can actually enable you to see farther than if you only stare straight ahead. Understanding the past can help you identify themes, patterns, and beliefs that both underscore why you care about certain matters now and explain why making them better into the future is such a high priority. (Kouzes and Posner 2012, 106)

This need to identify with a shared past in order to arrive at a shared future explains Exodus, chapter 13.

Upon their deliverance from Egypt, the first thing Moses implements is a pattern of remembrance. He establishes the first celebration of this newly forming nation. He does so because he does not want them to forget that it is God who has brought them to this place of freedom, and it will be God who ultimately brings them to their Promised Land. Moses looks forward to the life of this nation and reminds them to remember: *"This observance will be for you like a sign on your hand and a reminder on your forehead that this law of the LORD is to be on your lips. For the LORD brought you out of Egypt with his mighty hand. You must keep this ordinance at the appointed time year after year"* (Exodus 13:9-10). The implementation of the moments of remembrance signifies the work of Moses to establish the shared story of the Israelites. These people are a nation, but they are also a family. They were slaves, but they are now free. They were small and weak, but they are now numerous and strong. And lest they should forget how they became a nation, a family, free, and strong, Moses will establish the story of who they are from the very outset of the nation.

In January of 1999 at our first service as the pastoral couple for New Life Wesleyan Church, and in the face of the financial and growth challenges everyone knew we were facing, I issued an invitation. "I am inviting all of you to a black-tie dinner that we will hold in November. At that dinner, we will celebrate the fact that God has seen us through this year and brought us out of our troubles." Now, I am no prophet, but I just had a sense that God was about to do something incredible. I knew that if they could catch the idea that it was God who had done it from the beginning, they would have a shared story of deliverance and power. The power of God working through us would become our shared story. As November approached, I went out and bought a tuxedo and my wife bought a beautiful formal dress. We secured the services of an excellent caterer, and we held our dinner. The church had not missed a single bill, had not missed a single payroll, the pastors were full-time employed at the church, and the church paid for the dinner! During that event, we took up an offering. The offering was for missions and was spent entirely outside of the church. We celebrated the goodness of God and made it part of our story. Most years, though not all, since then, we have held our annual celebration of New Life Banquet, at least among those at the original campus. Every year, we recall and retell the story. We do this because it is our story. It gives identity and meaning to who we are as a church. I fully concur with the following:

> I believe our identities are formed by stories told to us, about us, and around us. We are *living texts*, formed by multiple, interweaving, competing, and, sometimes, conflicting stories that we receive from our culture via our parents, other adults, our peers, the media, and congregational life. Stories about race, gender, theology, generational differences, sexual orientation, ethnicity, and class work consciously and unconsciously to form our identity. Stories also teach us values, ethics, and meaning. Stories help us know who we are and who we are not; they create boundaries, or *borders*, for us. Identity development can be thought of as the process of refining, editing (*redacting*), and *authoring* one's own story in conversation with others. (Lewis 2008, 5)

It is imperative as leaders that we take hold of our story. Our church has a history, a story. Our future will be in many ways directed or at least affected by that story. If we can decide early on what that narrative should, or at least could, look like, we can begin the process of developing within our people a shared sense of destiny and purpose. The simple truth is that our people and our work will have a narrative. If we don't do the work of establishing that narrative, then someone else will do that work for us. They will look over what they can see of our work and progress, and they will write the narrative that they glean from what they can see. That narrative will be lacking. It will lack the heart of the issue. An onlooker can see what we did, but they cannot see why we did it. They do not always see the heart of the leader or the depth of the conviction. There are so many cases of people who simply know what we did, but they have no idea why. When we take charge of our own stories, we have the opportunity to make sure that those who follow us, as a group or individual, know more than just the "what" of our history. They can know the "why."

New Life Church is now a network of congregations. People have asked me why I took this approach to spreading the gospel. While I have many very good reasons why, there is a core part to my story that is not visible from the surface. Most of my life has been spent in the constant fear that I will ultimately mess things up. For some reason, whether it was the difficult teen years or the insecurity of my first years in ministry, I have just never had the confidence that normally seems to accompany the leader of such a large organization. Therefore, when the church began to grow, I was haunted by the fear that I would mess it up. So I decided to plant another church. That way if I messed up this one, that one could still thrive. It seemed to work, so we did it again. Don't get me wrong; there is a wonderful strategy that God has given to us for church expansion and multiplication. We intend to saturate our areas with the good news of Jesus and multiply churches until folks can't get anywhere without running into a church and church people. But inwardly, down where no one else could see, there is caveat to my story. I tell that part of the story because people need to understand the "why" behind the "how." If they don't, they will be tempted to be impressed by my doings. When looking a little deeper, they can fully realize that it was all God's doing. I'm just trying to protect what God has done for me.

The Israelites were slaves, and that is part of the story.

The Israelites' leader is a murderer, and that is part of the story.

The Israelites were wanderers, and that is part of the story.

New Life is a failed church building project, and that is part of the story.

Pastor Mike lives in fear of messing up, and that is part of the story.

The common thread in all these stories is a God who does not give up on insecure, failed, wandering, murderous, slaves. Instead, He calls them His own and builds into them a shared story.

Israel's story.

The church's story.

New Life's story.

Pastor Mike's story.

HIS story.

GIVE PEOPLE THE SPACE TO LEARN FAITH GRADUALLY

> *Then the LORD said to Moses, "Tell the Israelites to turn back and encamp near Pi Hahiroth, between Migdol and the sea. They are to encamp by the sea, directly opposite Baal Zephon. Pharaoh will think, 'The Israelites are wandering around the land in confusion, hemmed in by the desert.' And I will harden Pharaoh's heart, and he will pursue them. But I will gain glory for myself through Pharaoh and all his army, and the Egyptians will know that I am the LORD."*
>
> *—Exodus 14:1-4*

Let's make an analogy to mountain climbing. Imagine watching a rock climber scale a cliff without a rope; if she falls, she dies. To the uninformed spectator, the climber looks bold and risk-seeking, if not foolhardy. But suppose that climber is on a climb that to *her* appears eminently doable, well within her range of ability. From the climber's perspective, she has no doubts that, with proper training and concentration, she can make the climb. To her, the climb is not too risky. It *does* stimulate her to know that if she falls, she dies; but she has confidence in her ability. The highly visionary companies in

setting bold BHAGs [Big Hairy Audacious Goal] are
much like that climber.

—Jim Collins and Jerry I. Porras, *Built To Last*

God has Moses lead the Israelites down a path to the
Red Sea avoiding the shorter and more obvious route through
Philistine country. There seems to be two reasons for this
departure from what might be expected. These two reasons
ultimately lead the Israelites to experience one of the greatest
uplifts of which a new movement and new nation could ever
dream.

Early Hardships are the Most Dangerous

*"When Pharaoh let the people go, God did not lead them on the road
through the Philistine country, though that was shorter. For God said,
'If they face war, they might change their minds and return to Egypt.'"*
(Exodus 13:17)

God understands something about His people that many
leaders miss. Too much pain too early can kill the momentum
of any team. Change and progress require pain and sacrifice.
This is an absolute truth. However, great leaders understand
that the level of pain and sacrifice required of those on the team
must be, to the best of the leader's ability, managed. Sometimes
choices can be made as to what risk or which challenge will be
faced first. When those choices exist, good leaders understand

the need to capture the wins early and, as far as possible, pay the higher prices as the faith of the group grows. One simply cannot expect a mature response out of an immature group, or a faithful response out of an inexperienced group. "People who've never had the experience of being on a winning team often fail to realize that *every* team member must pay a price. I think some of them think that if others work hard, they can coast to their potential. But that is never true" (Maxwell 2001, 137). As these Israelites were leaving slavery in Egypt, they had seen God do great things to the Egyptians. They had seen God do great things for Moses. They had not yet really come to understand God's willingness to do great things for them. That lesson needed to be learned before they would ever be able to sustain any lengthy, bloody battle. They will eventually face the Philistines over and over again, but now is not the time.

Lingering Threats are the Most Discouraging

"But I [God] will gain glory for myself through Pharaoh and all his army, and the Egyptians will know that I am the LORD." (Exodus 14:4)

There are few things more discouraging than a lingering, unaddressed threat. The knowledge that some person, entity, or flaw which can bring destruction is allowed to sustain within or around an individual or organization, will bring a lingering fear and dread. These types of lingering threats must be identified and confronted. When they are allowed to linger, they erode the confidence and peace of the organization and leadership team. They can even erode the confidence of the leader. Brutal honesty about the lingering armies that surround you is required in order to practice top-level leadership. As God directs Moses toward the inevitable next conflict, He makes a choice. He chooses against the Philistine invasion and chooses a showdown with the Egyptian King. Why? It doesn't take a great deal of insight to realize that the Philistines really have no beef with the Israelites. Their departure from Egypt likely improves Philistine life by weakening the Egyptian nation. Egypt, however, has a huge incentive to come after the Israelites, and that incentive will not soon fade away. Brutal honesty is imperative when choosing and managing conflicts. "The good-to-great companies displayed two distinctive forms of disciplined thought. The first, and the topic of this chapter, is that they infused the entire process with the brutal facts of reality…. You absolutely cannot make a series of good decisions without first confronting the brutal facts" (Collins 2001, 69-70).

Established Confidence is the Most Empowering

By leading the nation of Israel down to the Red Sea, God sets up a showdown with the Egyptian King. He knows that the Pharaoh will misinterpret the *"wandering"* of the Israelites and assume they are lost and confused. He knows that the King will pursue them to the edge of the sea and attempt to either destroy or return them to Egypt. He understands that by letting them go, He has effectively dismissed the workforce of His nation and significantly reduced the power to produce, build, and expand His kingdom. He now realizes that His nation has been plundered as the Israelites took the wealth of Egypt with them on their way out the door. This King has every reason to pursue and fight the newborn nation of Israel. God knows that the lingering fear of being chased by the Egyptians will ultimately serve as a drag on the progress of His people toward His plan. Therefore, he sets up a showdown in which God will show the Israelites that He will fight for them. He will teach them that there are no armies that can successfully pursue and overtake them as long as God is protecting them. He will give them a short-term win that will have a long-term effect on the way they think, act, plan, and proceed.

> In successful change efforts, empowered people create short-term wins—victories that nourish faith in the change effort, emotionally reward the hard workers, keep the critics at bay, and build momentum. Without sufficient wins that are visible, timely, unambiguous, and meaningful to others, change efforts inevitably run into serious problems. (Kotter and Cohen 2002, 123)

WHEN GOD IS WITH YOU ... BET THE FARM!

> *Then Moses stretched out his hand over the sea, and all that night the LORD drove the sea back with a strong east wind and turned it into dry land.*
>
> —*Exodus 14:21*

On any team, in any organization, all responsibility for success and failure rests with the leader. *The leader must own everything in his or her world.* There is no one else to blame.

—Jocko Willink and Leif Babin, *Extreme Ownership*

I have often marveled at this point in the story of Moses' life. God has led them to the edge of this Red Sea. He has left them hemmed in and now trapped by an angry king and his army. Pharaoh has nothing left to lose. If he returns the Hebrews to Egypt, that's a win as it returns the workforce to his nation. It is also a win if he simply slaughters them all here and carries back the wealth of his nation to his people. For Moses, the math is entirely different. Moses has everything to lose. Today is life or death, at least for him. On this day, God will either deliver the nation of Israel, or Moses and some percentage of the Israelites will die here beside the Red Sea. It is with this realization that Moses gets his orders from God.

"Then the LORD said to Moses, 'Why are you crying out to me? Tell the Israelites to move on. Raise your staff and stretch out your hand over the sea to divide the water so that the Israelites can go through the sea on dry ground" (Exodus 14:15-16). I have to admit, I still chuckle a bit internally every time I read that. When I hear the voice of the Lord in this passage, in my head He sounds so baffled at Moses' hesitation. "Just lift up your staff and walk! What is so hard about that?" From God's perspective, the Red Sea is no barrier. From Moses' perspective, it's a pretty extreme obstacle! God has a plan and when He is done, both God and Moses will hold significantly higher levels of respect and authority.

"Raise your staff"

The entire nation is looking intently at Moses. The army of Pharaoh is bearing down with bloodthirsty vengeance on their minds. The only way to escape is through the water. God wants Moses to climb up on some high point, in front of everyone, and raise his staff BEFORE any of the water begins to recede. This is a really tough ask. I know that, for many, it seems that Moses' responsibility here is simple, but it really isn't. The shepherd's staff that Moses is about to lift above the water represents his leadership, his influence, and his authority. God has just asked him to put all of that on the line for a promised result that has never been seen before and seems entirely impossible now. Furthermore, Moses doesn't get a test run at this. Can't you just hear Moses' thoughts? "OK God, can I just run to the creek over there, just you and me, and make sure this works? You know, just to be sure I do my part right?" But no such run-through is allowed. Moses must do this thing, in public, and now!

Leadership is like that. Leaders have to take the risks first. It is in the risk that the miracle is released. "Like all leaders, Moses possesses the rod, and all he has to do is believe that he has the power, the ability, to lead. Once he does, he has to wield that power effectively; he has to be willing to act" (Cohen 2007, 25). When God calls leaders to great moments, He calls them to put it all on the line. Our reputations, our leadership, our authority must all be front and center before God will begin parting the waters. It matters that we are willing to do all of this publicly. When we announce to the people what God has said He is going to do and then step out in the faith that God will actually do it, no one is tempted to give the leader credit for God's miracle. It must have been painfully obvious to the Israelites that Moses had no chance of parting those waters. Having never seen God move on their behalf in such a miraculous manner, the people likely thought they were done for. Some were perhaps already just walking toward the Egyptians ready to surrender and beg for mercy! But Moses trusted in God's power even when his personal capacity was so obviously insufficient.

"I will gain glory through Pharaoh and all his army"

In the end, God is the one who gets the glory when we

do the right thing. It is an amazing thing to know that God is willing to work through us. He is willing to have His power flow through us to accomplish His will. That is all that happened on this day. It is painfully obvious to the Israelites that Moses is insufficient for this work, and their reaction to him is not kind. "The people, facing crisis in the desert, immediately question Moses's authority and leadership, and voice the desire to return to Egypt" (Cohen 2007, 40). When God chooses to use His chosen leader, He will always get the glory. The leader will gain the authority of being the one through which God's glory was practiced. What God bestows on Moses on this day is moral authority for times of crisis. "Eloquent speeches about common values aren't nearly enough, however. Leaders' deeds are far more important than their words when constituents want to determine how serious leaders really are about what they say" (Kouzes and Posner 2012, 17). Throughout the rest of the Exodus story, the people of Israel must trust that their God will deliver them. That trust must be embodied in the person of Moses. When Moses shows faith, the people find courage. That pattern begins right here, right now.

In our day, things really haven't changed much. Our people expect us to be the first to step out into the dangerous arena of faith. They expect to see us raising the staff of leadership in the faith that God will come through. When they witness our faith accompanied by God's faithfulness, they can act in the courage of knowing that the same God who came through last time will come through this time. Although our people realize that we are only human like them, they also trust that we hear from God. In that knowledge, they will find the courage to act, the faith to follow, and the security to rest. As Moses lifted his staff over the waters, no doubt somewhat fearful and uncertain about what would transpire, he did so with faith, *"and all that night the LORD drove the sea back with a strong east wind and turned it into dry land"* (Exodus 14:21).

DON'T FEAR ENDINGS ... RECOGNIZE BEGINNINGS

> *Then the LORD said to Moses, "Stretch out your hand over the sea so that the waters may flow back over the Egyptians and their chariots and horsemen." Moses stretched out his hand over the sea, and at daybreak the sea went back to its place. The Egyptians were fleeing toward it, and the LORD swept them into the sea. The water flowed back and covered the chariots and horsemen—the entire army of Pharaoh that had followed the Israelites into the sea. Not one of them survived.*
>
> *—Exodus 14:26-28*

First, the target is not always where we think it is; the actual shape and actions of a missional congregation are difficult to bring into focus at the beginning of this process.

—Alan J. Roxburgh and Fred Romanuk
The Missional Leader

New beginnings are always accompanied by endings. Sometimes those endings can be traumatic. Just as the future is not the past, the progress of the past is not the progress of the future. Quite often, I will speak with a pastor or ministry leader who is taking on a new task. Normally this new task involves taking the reigns of leadership for an existing church or ministry. Inevitably, the leader is looking to effect change without causing conflict, but there is an inherent problem in that goal. Change naturally brings conflict. "People basically don't like change. But if a church has been operating a program or process the same way for thirty years, then it may be time to look at what is happening" (Petersen et al. 2010, 211). These statements amuse me. If a church has been operating the same way for the past 30 years, or operating a single program the same way for the past 30 years, it is not correct to suggest that "it may be time to look at what is happening." It would be correct to say that it is ABSOLUTELY time to look at what is happening. My most common advice to pastors who take on new roles in existing congregations is shocking and must be applied carefully and lovingly. "Most of the folks you have are not the ones you need. Current-level people will not lead your next-level church. It all has to change."

As part of the ministry of New Life Network, we occasionally take leadership in failing or discontinued congregations. When we enter the new work, there are always two things we do. We close the church for a predetermined amount of time, and we disband the church board. These two things must sound very harsh to you as you read these words. At the very least, they don't sound as acceptable as "it may be time to look at what is happening." The truth is that the leadership in that congregation has already been tested, and it failed the test. In speaking with a friend who took over failing hotels, John Maxwell asked about their normal procedure:

> Don said that whenever his people went into an organization to take it over, they always started by doing two things. First, they trained all the staff to improve their level of service to the customers, and second, they fired the leader. When he told me that, I was surprised. "You always fire him?" I asked. "Every time?" "That's right. Every time," he said. "Don't you talk to the person first—to check him out to see if he's a good leader?" I said. "No," He answered. "If he'd been a good leader, the organization wouldn't be in the mess it's in." (Maxwell 2007, 8-9)

The same truth that is at work in this secular example applies to the church. The complication is that often that lack of leadership capacity is not limited to the departing pastor. Most often within churches that have been in decline for decades, and that unfortunately describes many churches, there is a deep lack of leadership capacity within the board. These volunteers who have sacrificed for their church, often built the church with their own hands, invested their own money, or have been part of the congregation their entire lives lack nothing in passion, commitment, sacrifice, and desire to make the church better. What they lack is the capacity to see beyond what has always been.

If we were to apply the same lens to Moses and the Israelites, these long-term, well-meaning church folks would be like those Israelites who continually complained: *"Was it because there were no graves in Egypt that you brought us to the desert to die? What have you done to us by bringing us out of Egypt? Didn't we say to you in Egypt, 'Leave us alone; let us serve the Egyptians'? It would have been better for us to serve the Egyptians than to die in the desert"* (Exodus 14:11-12). I am not convinced that these Israelites were bad people. They were afraid, and they had a distinct preference for what was known in the past over what was unknown and untested in the future. They were blaming Moses for God's plan. The reason for this is that they really couldn't blame God for it. Since God was too … well, God … to blame, they blamed Moses for their fear and discomfort. They longed for the slow death of slavery over the slow rise of freedom. Honestly, those types of people are still around today.

For those people, there must be an ending before there can be a beginning. Now I must point out that the complaint I listed from Exodus 14 occurs before God splits the sea and rescues the nation through the waters. Even after that, these types of complaints arise, but there is one significant difference. Returning to Egypt is not a realistic option after the Red Sea. By destroying the Egyptian army in the Red Sea, God effectively burned the bridge back to Egypt for the Israelites. Consider it for a moment. The Egyptians blame the Israelites for the plagues, the death of their first-born sons, the plundering of their wealth, and now the death of literally thousands of soldiers. There is no logical pathway back, and that is important. Given the option of returning to the comfort and relative safety of known slavery, many would leave the difficult path of freedom behind. These are not bad people, unintelligent people, or unfaithful people; they are just afraid. Often, they are not even afraid for themselves. They fear for their families, their children, their parents, and their communities. They fear that the security and familiarity of Egypt will never again be found in this new land. Here's the difficult truth. For them, it won't. The kind of security and familiarity they are looking for will not be found again for another generation. In the case of the Israelites, the delay is due to their lack of faith when they first arrive at the border of the Promised Land. (We will deal with that in a later entry.) In the case of so many churches that need so much change, the kind of nostalgia that these folks are looking for cannot be found again in this generation. They trade that for a new life, a new reality, and a new church. Whether they trade it willingly or they are forced to move on, what they yearn for is gone.

It is for this reason that so many leadership writers are so cautious when they talk about change.

> Times have changed. The Bill Gaither Trio, the gospel group, was big thirty years ago, and though many still enjoy them because they are very good, the style of song ministry has changed. The contemporary style of Generation Y (born after 1980) features lyrics that are more personal than theological and favors drums and guitars over the piano and organ. In some circles even the use of hymns has almost disappeared. But this is the music many today will listen to, and

church leaders have to pay attention to it. At the same time, they cannot ignore the preferences of older generations in trying to fashion a healthy blend of worship music. (Petersen et al. 2010, 211)

The problem becomes one of progress. With all possible respect and with a heart that breaks for close family that still attend churches that would love to have the Gaithers lead worship in their congregation, God did not blend the Israelites and the Egyptians. He did not keep some of their traditions that weren't abhorrent to God's holiness and simply integrate them into Jewish life. No. God led them to the Red Sea and once and for all washed the Egyptian right out of the Israeli. The nation of Egypt survived this ordeal, albeit horribly weakened. God did not destroy all evidence that the Egyptians ever existed; he simply started something new and definitively marked the end of the old and beginning of the new. In modern times, it means that God does not wipe out the use of hymns, organs, or Gaithers. He simply allows His church to march forward in a new sense toward a new day with theology intact (even restored). The idols of the past are dysfunctional for the future.

We need to stop fearing these Red Sea moments in the church. The only folks who ever risk drowning in these moments are the ones who are so afraid of the new change. These folks may remain in the midst of the waters with the Egyptians instead of following the people of Israel through to the other side. I often wonder if any of the Israelites perished that way on this night. I could imagine some of them longing so deeply for the comfort of Egyptian slavery that they ran back toward the armies of Egypt only to drown in the waters of God's new day. These endings are undoubtedly difficult and often traumatic, but they are nonetheless necessary.

Now, for you as the leader, when looking at those who wish to return to Egypt:

> **1. Work hard to understand the fear that causes many to long for the dysfunction of the past over the hope of the future.**
>
> **2. Never disparage or disregard them.**
>
> **3. Never see them as anything less than God's children and His loving creation.**
>
> **4. Never intentionally hurt them.**

When you are moving forward in God's calling for you:

> **1. Never fail to raise your staff over the waters.**
>
> **2. Never fear to lead your people through the waters.**
>
> **3. Never leave anyone in the waters.**
>
> **4. Never fear allowing the waters to close over your past and effectively wash the slave out of the people who are now free.**

When we learn to embrace the endings brought about by Red Sea moments, we can finally progress toward our generational promised land of God's best and brightest. That does not mean we can ignore or disrespect the history of those who got us this far, which brings us to the next entry. Please note that these two MUST be taken together in order to avoid unnecessary pain and hurt. The future is where God is taking us ... but the past is how He got us here!

RESULTS MATTER ... FOR A LONG TIME!

> *But the Israelites went through the sea on dry ground, with a wall of water in their right and on their left. That day the LORD saved Israel from the hands of the Egyptians, and Israel saw the Egyptians lying dead on the shore. And when the Israelites saw the mighty hand of the LORD displayed against the Egyptians, the people feared the LORD and put their trust in him and in Moses his servant.*
>
> *—Exodus 14:29-31*

One of the first things new leaders should do, preferably even before arriving on the field, is to study the history of the organization. This is important in any organization, but it is particularly crucial in the case of spiritual organizations such as churches, schools, and charities.... God does not work in a vacuum. He has been unfolding his plan since he began time. Much history as preceded the leader's arrival at the organization. Leaders are remiss if they make decisions as if there were no track record or history to their organization.

—Henry and Richard Blackaby, *Spiritual Leadership*

Understanding the past is an indispensable part of shaping the future. This Red Sea event is forever etched into the memory of the nation of Israel. The event is so pivotal that it is still mentioned in numerous places in the New Testament. Centuries pass and yet this one moment lingers. The lesson it taught is still core to the actual identity of the people of Israel. In fact, the entire Exodus narrative is intricately ingrained within the very understanding of what it means to be a Hebrew. "We are *living texts* formed by multiple, interweaving stories that we receive from multiple sources in our culture" (Lewis 2008, 19). If a new leader in a new setting fails to understand the narrative of the "living texts" she has just entered into, the results can be disastrous. While it is imperative that we embrace Red Sea moments, it is equally imperative that we understand history. The Red Sea may have washed the slave out of the people who are now free, but the reality that slavery was part of the fabric of the Israelite culture has never been lost. We must understand that Egypt did not begin as a place of slavery. It began as a place of deliverance and protection. Likewise, the traditions that we often must battle in order to make progress in today's church became traditional simply because they worked. They are still a part of the fabric of who we are as followers of Christ. Effective leaders are able to balance the important differences between celebrating the traditions of the past and utilizing the realities of the present, while progressing toward the promised land of the future.

Before we jump into these three areas of leadership, let's consider a conversation about how change actually functions these days:

> Discontinuous change and developmental change are not the same. Developmental is about more of what has been; it's change within a familiar paradigm. Examples are everywhere. One buys a new car or introduces drums or drama or video into a worship service; a book written about missional leadership has a familiar chapter on the need for high commitment to church membership rather than asking the deeper questions of membership and belonging. These instances are all about change *within* a world…. Discontinuous change is different. There is a wonderful IBM ad that captures something of what it means. A team of people evidently starting up a business, after working hard to develop an online marketing strategy, gather around a computer as their product goes online. They look hopefully and expectantly for the first Internet sale. When one comes through, they nervously look at each other, relieved that something has happened. Then ten more sales come through. Muted excitement runs through the anxious room. Then, suddenly, a hundred or so orders show up on the computer screen. The team is cheering and hugging one another in exultation; all their hard work has paid off. Then they stare at the screen, beyond disbelief: instead of hundreds of orders, which they couldn't have imagined in their wildest dreams, there are suddenly thousands. Everyone is overwhelmed.

> No one knows how to deal with this; it's outside their skills and expertise. They are at a loss to know what to do next. The organization has moved to a level of complexity that is beyond the team's skills and ability to address. In a period of discontinuous change, leaders suddenly find that the skills and capacities in which they were trained are of little use in addressing a new situation and environment. (Roxburgh and Romanuk 2006, 8-9)

As church leaders, we are often called to simultaneously deal with developmental change and discontinuous change. Even when we break free from the simpler form of developmental change and begin to run freely in the Wild West of discontinuous change, we must have some anchors that hold us to the core values that should and must remain if we are to lead a church and not simply lead a community group. Discontinuous change can confuse and alter the very definition of who we are and why we do what we do. This is the type of change many of us are facing these days. It is precisely the type of change that the Israelites were facing. "Discontinuous change is dominant in periods of history that *transform* a culture forever, tipping it over into something new. The Exodus stories are an example of a time when God tipped history in a new direction and in so doing transformed Israel from a divergent group of slaves into a new kind of people" (Roxburgh and Romanuk 2006, 7).

Celebrating Past Traditions

Simply put, tradition became traditional because it worked. Tradition does not rise to the level of theology. Let's be clear in our discussion of change. Our theology must remain, at its core, a static reality. God does not change. The God of the world, pre-Exodus, is the same God in the post-Exodus world and is the same God as today. What changes is the way He allows us to see and experience Him and the way He, through development and technology, allows us to see and experience each other. Times of discontinuous change are marked by profound differences in the way we understand our world, the way we see the other people in our world, and the way we engage with and discover new ideas and realities. By that definition, we are certainly living in a time of discontinuous change. No matter how rapidly culture changes in these times, our theology must remain intact. We must hold to our biblical understanding of Christ and His redemptive work with all tenacity and at all costs. At the same time, our methodology of sharing and multiplying the gospel of Christ must remain dynamic. The only way to keep our bearings in a time of discontinuous change is to remember and understand our past. The Israelites needed desperately to understand and remember their slavery in order to move forward in faith with their newfound, God-given freedom.

The children of Israel were in Egypt because it was where God sent them to find food and water during a devastating drought. The Joseph story actually articulates Egypt as a place of plenty and a place of salvation. The children of Jacob (children of Israel) were not settled into the slave barracks; they were placed there out of Joseph's love for them and God's provision for them (Genesis 45:10). Likewise, much of the tradition that enslaves many churches and Christians today came into being for beautiful and meaningful reasons. These traditions need to be understood for what they brought to the table at the time and what they communicate to the faithful even today. Every movement and every congregation have their traditions. Before a leader sets out to destroy them all, it is imperative that he or she understands why they are there in the first place. Discontinuous change may demand that they be removed and replaced, or simply forgotten. Theological purity and understanding may demand that they remain and be defended throughout the storm of discontinuous change. The leader must do the work of understanding past traditions so that he or she can celebrate those that merit celebration and terminate those that simply propagate slavery.

Utilizing Present Reality

In every present, no matter how dynamic or transitional that present may be, there is a reality that is right here and right now. As leaders, we must speak into that reality for it is the real world our people live in. If we spend all of our time defending the traditions of the past, our people are lost with no tools for living in the present. Likewise, if we spend all of our time defining the church of the future, our people are unprepared for the world they will face when they set foot outside the walls of our church or small group. We must understand the past, prepare for the future, but equip our people to live in the present. At New Life, we often have people attend our church from more of a High Church liturgical background. The churches they come from practice beautiful and sometimes ancient forms of worship that leave the folks in the pews empty as to what to do when they leave the church. While I find these High Church rituals to be stunning and beautiful in their richness and history, they do little to help a 24-year old navigate the increasingly odd dating scene, or a 48-year old navigate the kind of depressing realization of mid-life. Those traditions have meaning and those rituals have deep significance, but God's Word can do so much more if it is released from bondage to the past or future. God is not the God that was, nor is He the God that will be. God is the God who eternally and invariably IS. Remember the past and prepare for the future, but bring the God who always IS to the present reality of your people, right where they are.

Progressing Toward the Future

It's hard to say with certainty what the future holds for any of our institutions. The Internet is challenging the very definition of who we are and how we accomplish things. The church is not alone in this challenging reality. I sit on the board of trustees for a Christian University, and online education is a real challenge that we must become part of or we won't exist in the next generation. Brick and mortar stores are increasingly facing the challenges of competing with online sales outlets that can bypass the tremendous expense of retail presentation through the digital world of online presentation. What once required millions of dollars for brick, mortar, wood, and wires now only requires a good camera and a skilled web designer. Churches are facing the same daunting reality. While we cannot predict what the church will look like 100 years from now, we know that Christ will still be the answer for humans in need of forgiveness.

I honestly don't know how every leader intends to prepare for this brave new world, but I intend to attempt to do it all. I am not convinced that personal gatherings in singular locations of large groups of people will cease to exist in the next generation or two. But I could be wrong. So we will do online church. I am not convinced that everyone is going to go to church online. But I could be wrong. So we will continue to plant and foster church communities that meet in every community where God gives us favor. I am not convinced that all young people are going to relocate to urban centers. But I could be wrong. So we will make every attempt to enter the urban center with congregations and online opportunities. You see where this is going. I'm just not smart enough to know exactly what the future will be like. So as God gives us strength, resource, and opportunity, we will attempt to do it all.

In short, change is inevitable. Tomorrow will never look like today. As we face that inevitable change, we should do so with a deep respect, understanding, and even reverence for our history. We should do so with a clear-minded and wide-ranging eye toward whatever the future may look like. Most importantly, we should do so with an unwavering commitment to bring Christ (the God who always is) into the current reality of the people God has called us to serve.

INTEGRITY MATTERS

> *Then Moses led Israel from the Red Sea and they went into the Desert of Shur. For three days they traveled in the desert without finding water. When they came to Marah, they could not drink its water because it was bitter. (That is why the place is called Marah.) So the people grumbled against Moses, saying, "What are we to drink?" Then Moses cried out to the LORD and the LORD showed him a piece of wood. He threw it into the water, and the water became fit to drink. There the LORD issued a ruling and instruction for them and put them to the test. He said, "If you listen carefully to the LORD your God and do what is right in his eyes, if you pay attention to his commands and keep all his decrees, I will not bring on you any of the diseases I brought on the Egyptians, for I am the LORD, who heals you." Then they came to Elim, where there were twelve springs and seventy palm trees, and they camped there near the water.*
>
> *—Exodus 15:22-27*

Self-identity is the foundation on which everything else is constructed. Missional leadership depends on the leader's maturity, trust, and integrity. Well-developed capabilities in the other three areas are important, but they support lasting change only if the congregation has a high level of confidence in the leader's character. These attributes are placed first because they are the ticket to missional leadership.

—Alan J. Roxburgh and Fred Romanuk
The Missional Leader

We all know the old adage that "everything rises and falls on leadership," and that is true. In reality, leadership almost always rises and falls on the issue of integrity. If it is true that leadership is influence, then a person who is effective at what they do may lack influence if they fail to show integrity in how they do it. Therefore, integrity is core to leadership, especially in church leadership. "The church is the arena in which the integrity of those using power comes most clearly into focus" (Schmidt 2006, 149). Integrity plays out in different ways largely based on the role of leadership that a person is given. In the account we have here from Exodus 15, we find God giving a new level of definition and expectation to the people of Israel. He also gives them a new promise, if they learn to act with integrity. Let's look at how this event marked all of those involved.

Moses Shows Integrity through Humility

When Moses is approached by the people concerning the lack of water, they do not exactly approach him kindly or gently. They approached him "grumbling." They insisted that he tell them where and how he was going to provide the water that they needed to move forward. Now, it's not like Moses needed to be informed about the lack of water. It is often amazing to me that people think leaders don't see the obvious. Of course, Moses knew that they needed water. It is likely that he has been leading them through the desert worried about finding water long before they saw it as a concern. In fact, Moses likely walked away from the Red Sea three days ago wondering where he would find enough water for all these people. But here they are having traveled for three days and all they find is a bitter mud hole called Mara. (According to Blue Letter Bible, the Hebrew word literally means "bitter.") In the midst of the people complaining (with good reason) and Moses not knowing what to do, the Bible says, *"Moses cried out to the LORD."* This is an important reaction for any leader to understand and ultimately apply. Moses surely was aware of the need for water. He was doing all he knew to do to find the water the people needed. He thought he had it all figured out, and then he found that the waters of Mara were, well, Mara. Now, he could have lashed out at those who were sarcastically "grumbling" at him. I suppose he would have had every right to just give them a piece of his mind. "Don't you know that I am aware of our need for water? What do you think I am doing up here? Washing camels? I'm trying! And by the way, I don't need all this attitude out of you!" I guess he could have done that, and I would be willing to venture a guess that he wanted to react that way. But he didn't. He could see the need of the people, and he knew that he lacked the answers they needed. So he did the right thing. In humility, knowing he had no answers, he cried out to God. He admitted his lack of capacity and sought the strength of the Father for an answer. He responded with integrity through his humility, and you better believe that people saw that happen. "Leaders with integrity inspire confidence in others because they can be trusted to do what they say they are going to do. They are loyal, dependable, and not deceptive. Basically, integrity makes a leader believable and worthy of our trust" (Northouse 2010, 21). Moses showed a humility that evidenced an integrity that made the people willing to follow.

The People Show Integrity through Obedience

God gives the people a directive: *"If you listen carefully to the LORD your God and do what is right in his eyes, if you pay attention to his commands and keep all his decrees ..."* The people are to show obedience to all that God has called them to observe. Through obedience, they will show integrity. Self-discipline is the requirement that He lays on His people, and that call is imperative as they all strive together to follow God's plan for reaching the Promised Land. Obedience will be crucial if they are to survive the desert and all of the other threats that will face this fledgling nation over the next 40 years. In fact, not much has changed. Obedience to God's commands and decrees is an essential part of any fully functioning church or Christian organization. The reason obedience is so crucial is really quite simple. "If you cannot discipline your life, spiritual crisis will loom" (Smith and Wright 2011, 220). When we, like the nation of Israel represent a spiritual organization, spiritual crisis is organizational crisis. Not unlike the nation of Israel, far too many instances exist which demonstrate the damage caused to individuals and the Kingdom of God when the people of God fail to follow in obedience the commands and decrees of God. His commands are not in place to keep us from enjoyment; they are in place to keep us from destruction. Our pathway to integrity is paved with His commands and decrees.

God Shows Integrity through Provision

"I will not bring on you any of the diseases I brought on the Egyptians, for I am the LORD, who heals you."

Ultimately God's integrity shows through to us through His faithfulness. He always provides. Though not always when we want or what we want, God never fails to provide what His servants need. "One of the lessons God's servants would learn was that he provides. The wilderness was a perfect place to teach this lesson, for this land was desolate, bereft of the provisions needed for a large group of people" (Lennox 2016, 105-106). Therefore, over and over again God provided for His people food, water, shelter, protection, light by night, and cloud by day; all of this, God simply provided for Israel. While this alone would have been enough, God was teaching a much deeper lesson. "Beyond healing the waters, God used this occasion to teach something to Moses and the Israelites:

God could heal them as easily as he healed these waters, if they would only trust and obey. To emphasize his point, God then led them to an oasis with plenty of water, where they set up camp" (Lennox 2016, 107).

We learn a lesson here about the roles each of us must play if we are ultimately going to find our own promised land.

Leaders must humble themselves, even in front of their people in order to clearly show that their dependence is on the God who provides and heals. Leaders, who fail to act humbly, miss the great leadership lessons of Scripture. Moses is not alone in this humility. We see this pattern repeated time and again culminating in Jesus, our Savior and Messiah, washing the feet of His disciples and ultimately dying for the sins of all mankind.

The people must learn to trust God and their leader and obey the commands God has given them. A lack of faith in God or in the leader is simply deadly to the progress of the community, as we will see in later entries.

Ultimately, God will remain faithful. When we trust in Him, we place our trust in the One who never fails. He is our example of faithfulness and integrity, and the more we learn to be like Him, the better off we will all become.

GATHER AN INNER CIRCLE
YOU CAN TRUST

The Amalekites came and attacked the Israelites at Rephidim. Moses said to Joshua, "Choose some of our men and go out to fight the Amalekites. Tomorrow I will stand on top of the hill with the staff of God in my hands." So Joshua fought the Amalekites as Moses had ordered, and Moses, Aaron and Hur went to the top of the hill. As long as Moses held up his hands, the Israelites were winning, but whenever he lowered his hands, the Amalekites were winning. When Moses' hands grew tired, they took a stone and put it under him and he sat on it. Aaron and Hur held his hands up—one on one side, one on the other—so that his hands remained steady till sunset. So Joshua overcame the Amalekite army with the sword. Then the LORD said to Moses, "Write this on a scroll as something to be remembered and make sure that Joshua hears it, because I will completely blot out the name of Amalek from under heaven." Moses built an altar and called it The LORD is my Banner. He said, "Because hands were lifted up against the throne of the LORD, the LORD will be at war against the Amalekites from generation to generation."

—Exodus 17:8-16

Not only does Moses need Joshua to lead the people in battle against Amalek, but his brother and nephew (Hur is Miriam's son, according to the rabbinic tradition) play key supportive roles as well. This is one of Moses's most important legacies as a leader—his recognition that he cannot succeed by acting alone. Like all leaders, he has no choice but to involve others in varying supportive roles.

—Norman J. Cohen
Moses and the Journey to Leadership

Numerous times in my life and ministry, I have faced rather dark periods. Now, I am not naturally given to bouts of deep and debilitating depression, but I can find myself in dark places where it is difficult to see a way through. These times normally come to me when I am tired and feeling the pressure of needing to "perform" or always be on top of my game in ministry. I can often feel that the careers of dozens of people are resting squarely on my shoulders. Most times, this realization is both humbling and invigorating. God has given me the opportunity to serve in such a way as to empower and release the fullness of not only my calling but also the calling of dozens of others. Sometimes when, for whatever reason, the load seems exceptionally heavy, I can enter into a dark and discouraging place. It is in these moments that I have learned to lean heavily on the strength of a core group of people with which God has richly blessed me. These people are irreplaceable rocks in the course of my life and leadership.

The simple fact is that I could not have made it this far without them.

And I am not unique.

Leaders desperately need the support of other leaders around them. While it may seem from a distance that they have it all together and can single-handedly take on any situation and win, that just isn't actually true. In the last half of chapter 17 of Exodus, we find Moses in such a situation. The Israelites have been attacked by the Amalekites, and Moses must respond in order to protect his people. He chooses to send Joshua out to fight against this enemy. Moses does not insist on leading the fight himself. Instead, he publicly recognizes and admits that Joshua is the right man for the job. He shows the humility to send someone else out to earn the victory. Furthermore, he empowers his young apprentice by allowing him to take some leadership of his own. He does not leave Joshua on his own. Moses climbs a hill and stands in clear view of the army of Israel, and he holds up his hand clearly displaying the staff that represents the presence and power of the Lord. However, Moses realizes a problem. When his hands are lifted, the army of Israel is winning. When his hands are lowered, the army of Amalek is winning.

But Moses gets tired.

Realizing what is going on, Moses's inner circle of supporters spring into action. Aaron and Hur hold up Moses' hands so that the Army of Israel can win the battle against

Amalek. Now, not only was Moses forced to admit that Joshua was the best man for the job of leading the army into battle, he also must admit that he lacks the strength, on his own, to represent the power and presence of the Lord to his people. It actually is a pretty tough day for a driven leader.

Leader, you need to learn from this. Perhaps as badly as you need a vision and talent, you need an inner circle. You need to surround yourself around people you can trust and to whom you can say anything. People you can call and just know that they will make room for you in their schedule, and when you arrive, they will clear the room, shut the door, hear you out, and help you through. These are not people who exist to stroke your ego or simply always say "yes" to you. These are people who love you enough to realize your weaknesses and help you accomplish what God has planned for your life. They will never be "yes men." They will always find a rock for you to sit on while they hold your hands high allowing you to reach God's calling for you.

> As a result of the support he receives, Moses's hands remain steady (yadav emunah) throughout the battle. The use of the word emunah is odd here, since it usually means "faith." Perhaps the point being made is that, because Moses himself is supported by Aaron, Hur, and even Joshua, his own faith is bolstered, even in the face of the enemy. All leaders need support to face and overcome challenges, and that support may reinforce their own resolve. (Cohen 2007, 86)

Once the battle was over, Moses was careful to teach the Israelites that the victory was not won because Moses kept his hands in the air. The staff of the Lord is no good luck charm that somehow brings power like a magician's wand. No, the victory belongs to God. It doesn't belong to Moses, Joshua, Aaron, or Hur, but it belongs to God. "According to the Kabbalah, the text of Jewish mysticism, humility means understanding that everything we are depends on the Lord. If we are a great leader, that means we are a channel for the Lord to accomplish his work" (Dilenschneider 2000, 44). No one is capable of being an effective channel for the work of the Lord alone. We need a strong inner circle that we can trust and lean on. When our hands get tired, they hold us up.

TAKE WISE COUNSEL

The next day Moses took his seat to serve as judge for the people, and they stood around him from morning till evening. When his father-in-law saw all that Moses was doing for the people, he said, "What is this you are doing for the people? Why do you alone sit as judge, while all these people stand around you from morning till evening?" Moses answered him, "Because the people come to me to seek God's will. Whenever they have a dispute, it is brought to me, and I decide between the parties and inform them of God's decrees and instructions." Moses' father-in-law replied, "What you are doing is not good."

—*Exodus 18:13-17*

It's easy for the needs or interests of insiders to ultimately drive the priorities of any organization. It's just the natural tendency of any group to become insider-focused. If you are surrounded long enough by people who think like you think, you will become more and more certain that's the *best* way to think. Over time you find yourself inclined to completely disregard the concerned voices of those positioned on the *outside*.

—Andy Stanley, Reggie Joiner, Lane Jones
Practices of Effective Ministry

I was attending a funeral at a small church with which I was familiar. Following the service would be a meal in the fellowship hall. Between the service and the meal, the pastor caught up with me. He knew who I was and knew that our church had experienced tremendous growth over the years. He also knew that we had successfully planted multiple churches around us. He said to me, "I'd love to pick your brain about congregational leadership." For the next 30-45 minutes, he talked to me about his ideas on leadership and then thanked me for the time we spent together. He let me know how much he had appreciated being able to "pick my brain." I simply looked at him, without having spoken much more than a sentence or two for the entire conversation, and said, "You're welcome," and we parted ways. I really can't even tell you how many times something like this has happened to me. A pastor comes to me with a concern, or I happen to be at a church where a pastor begins a discussion about leadership practices. The pastor then proceeds to talk without listening, or listening only to dismiss anything I may think or have to say. These people are not looking for leadership ideas or concepts they can apply to make themselves or their churches better; they simply desire the audience of someone they view as knowledgeable as a platform to repeat what they already believe. They aren't listening. Now, the truth is that I may or may not be able to give any insight that would be helpful to their situation or church. Honestly, it may be that I have nothing to offer. However, if you don't listen or attempt to receive what I have to say, you will never know.

Looking back, I can say that I have rarely been guilty of this. Sure, there have been moments when I didn't want to hear what was being said to me so I argued against it. There have been moments where in my own shortsightedness, I missed the opportunity to actually shut my mouth and learn. However, as a whole, I try hard to hear what people are saying to me and consider the possibility that it might make a difference in the way I do ministry. This is an incredibly important practice. The reason for its importance is very simple. It's really difficult to see something from a broad angle when you are sitting in the very center of it. I once heard someone suggest that if you are so close to a wall that your nose is touching it, you will be unable to see the doorway that is perhaps as little as four feet away from you. You will feel trapped and helpless. If you could only back up a few inches, you will immediately see the obvious escape route. Ministry can do that to us. It can blind us to other possibilities. We can be so close to what is wrong, our noses touching the wall, that we cannot see the answer that is obvious to everyone else. The only way out of this dilemma is to listen to the perspective of outsiders who can see what we can't or don't want to see.

Moses is facing such a moment in Exodus 18. He has been doing leadership in a particular way for a while now and it seems, at least to Moses, to be working. The process is not complicated. Moses goes out in the morning and sits in the center of the people. Anyone who has a dispute or a concern comes to him, explains the problem, and looks to him for a declaration or decision. It's all very effective, or at least it would be if there weren't an entire nation looking for answers! With some estimates as high as three million people who are following Moses at this point, you can imagine that the line waiting to talk to Moses would make your local Department of Motor Vehicles look downright efficient! It must have been exhausting. Scripture says that Moses started in the morning and they were still standing in line in the evening! At about this time, Moses' father-in-law, Jethro, comes to visit. He walks out and sees this spectacle and what must have been a never-ending line of people with grievances waiting to talk to Moses. He tries the gentle approach. "Whatcha doin'?" Moses, seemingly oblivious to the ridiculous nature of what is going on, just explains that the people want him to decide their differences. So Jethro must take a more direct approach to the problem: *"What you are doing is not good."*

Far too many leaders are seemingly caught in a cycle of *"not good"* leadership practice. There could be a number of reasons for this. Let's consider a couple.

Trapped in Tradition

While this nation of Israel is still very young and just developing its own identity and traditions, there seems be one tradition that has established itself almost instantly. Everyone goes to Moses for answers. Honestly, this is an understandable impulse for this young nation. The Israelites have watched as God spoke to Moses and empowered him throughout the plagues and ultimately at the parting of the Red Sea. Therefore, anyone who really wants to know what God thinks about a dispute wants to get that answer from Moses. He seems to be the one with the direct line. So Moses agrees to be the ultimate and seemingly only judge. While this is a bad choice on Moses' part, it is, again, understandable. The other elders of the people have been working with the Egyptians all these years. There may well be mistrust or a lack of understanding as to how to function outside of slavery among those elders. So Moses sits and judges the people all day. However, this practice that has become (in a very short amount of time) traditional is not sustainable.

The struggle with traditional ways of doing things is very real, and we have discussed it numerous times already in this text. Let me remind us how we get to a place like this. Tradition becomes traditional because it worked. God obviously speaks to Moses, and Moses is obviously able to apply what God says to the day-to-day workings of society. Moses has a connection to God that gives him a power that no one else has, so Moses as a judge seems to be working (at least for those that can get to him). Again, it is not sustainable. "Every institution is vulnerable, no matter how great. No matter how much you've achieved, no matter how far you've gone, no matter how much power you've garnered, you are vulnerable to decline. There is no law of nature that the most powerful will inevitably remain at the top. Anyone can fall and most eventually do" (Collins

2009, 8). Moses cannot continually be the only arbiter of God's truth. Even though what God has done through him to this point is incredible, even unprecedented, it cannot be sustained. When we finally realize that our traditions are not sustainable, we must begin to consider changes that can take us into the future. However, sometimes we don't.

Blinded by Adoration

Let's be honest. While it must have been exhausting for Moses to sit all day and judge between the Israelites, it must have felt good to know that everyone believed in him and needed him. Moses was always the center of attention, and it felt good. This lonely shepherd was now a superstar. This is a massive pitfall for leaders. The more success a leader experiences, the more adoration that leader is shown. Adoration feels good. It can blind a leader to the weaknesses that exist and leave that leader stuck in an unsustainable reality. Like any addiction, adoration can take hold of the desires of the leader and leave them trapped in a codependency that is destructive to both the leader and the organization. This is precisely where Moses finds himself. Cohen describes the situation perfectly.

> Moses is convinced that only he can play all the major roles, as we see in his reply to his father-in-law: "It is because the people come to me to inquire of God. When they have a dispute, it [necessarily] comes before me, and I decide between an individual and his neighbor, and I make known the laws and

teachings of God" (18:15-16). The haughty tone of Moses's reply betrays his sense that only he can judge, teach, and lead the People of Israel, and surely only he is uniquely qualified to intercede on behalf of the people before God. It is as if Moses were saying to Jethro: "I realize that you are concerned because I have undertaken a dual responsibility, both to judge and to teach. You feel that it would be prudent to appoint other judges. But how can I do so? When people have a dispute, an ordinary judge will have no way to determine who is speaking the truth. Only I can do that through my prophetic powers." Moses's ego truly gets in the way of recognizing what is in the best interests of his people and their future. Leaders must acknowledge that they cannot control and run everything. What ultimately makes leaders successful, among many crucial traits, is their humility, even as they embody the highest ideals and standards of the group. (Cohen 2007, 90-91)

As Moses looks at the current reality around him, he is not wrong to recognize that God has uniquely empowered him and is uniquely communicating with him. Where he goes wrong is to assume that this means he is the only hope for the people. The people want Moses to decide, and Moses wants the people to want him to decide. So we enter into a dysfunctional codependency that is leaving everyone exhausted and frustrated. Many leaders, and especially pastors, face this very situation today. It is obvious that the Holy Spirit is speaking through the pastor to the people, and so all of the people want the pastor to personally deal with all of their problems. If the pastor is honest, the pastor likes the fact that the people desire his or her wisdom and guidance. As the church grows, there just isn't enough of the pastor to go around. Now a choice has to be made. If Moses does not change his approach, the nation of Israel will fail. They will ultimately descend into frustration, anger, and disillusionment leaving Moses incapable of leading and too burnt out to find answers. The nation of Israel will die in the desert. Church growth cannot continue if the pastor must do it all. In order for growth and progress to continue, leadership and control must be shared.

The advice of Jethro may not be from inside the ranks, and it may not be what Moses or the people want to hear, but it is nonetheless good advice.

COMMUNICATE VISION

> *Listen now to me and I will give you some advice, and may God be with you. You must be the people's representative before God and bring their disputes to him. Teach them his decrees and instructions, and show them the way they are to live and how they are to behave.*
>
> *—Exodus 18:19-20*

If it is true that great visions inspire great people and great organizations, the crucial task for leaders is to develop the loftiest vision possible for their organizations.

—Henry and Richard Blackaby, *Spiritual Leadership*

I once came across a question that has become foundational in my life and leadership. As the church I pastor was growing, a mentor of mine presented me with this question: What can you not, not do?

That question intrigued me from the beginning. First of all, it just reads funny and seems to require a bit of digging just to understand. As I unpacked it, I realized that I was dealing with the question of ultimate priorities. There are some things as a pastor that I simply must do myself. There are some things as a leader that I simply must do myself. But, honestly, the list of things that I cannot not do is rather short. The larger the organization or the church becomes, the shorter that list becomes. In fact, there are many things that fall into the category of things I should not do because others on my team do them better. No matter how large or expansive the organization, there are some things that the leaders must do personally. Vision is one of those things. It is the job of the leader to look forward into the future and with Spirit-led vision, see what is not yet. That vision of where the organization or the church can go is the vision that God gives to the leader. It is the responsibility of the leader to vocalize that vision and then structure the team to accomplish that vision. The vision must determine the structure of the organization, not the other way around. Simply put, if you don't know where you are going and you don't know what you are going to do when you get there, you cannot possibly build an organization that succeeds. Understanding the end goal is imperative. In Moses' case, the end goal is clear; the people of Israel are going to the Promised Land. When they arrive, the mission will be clear. They must drive out the current inhabitants and establish the nation of Israel, God's people, in this Promised Land, God's land. The question now is how will Moses get them there?

Jethro, in his advice to Moses, is clearly telling Moses what he should not be doing. Moses should not be deciding small and petty disputes between the Israelites and their neighbors. *"What you are doing is not good."* He also is clear about what Moses should be doing. *"Teach them his decrees and instructions, and show them the way they are to live and how they are to behave."* The message could not be more simple: "Moses, you figure out where this nation is going and what they must accomplish once they arrive there, and then teach the people how to get where they are going and become what they are becoming." Moses was faced with learning to envision the future for his people in such a way that they would want to go where God was sending them, would be willing to endure the journey to get there, and willing to fight for the ultimate goal that would lay at the end. This is no small task.

> Enlisting others is all about igniting passion for a purpose and moving people to persist against great odds. To get extraordinary things done in organizations, you have to go beyond reason, engaging the hearts as well as the minds of your constituents. You start by understanding their strongest yearnings for something meaningful and significant. (Kouzes and Posner 2012, 129-130)

A Compelling Vision: Envision the future in such a way that people want to go where God is sending them.

Vision that works must be able to capture the hearts and minds of the people who are following you. Setting the goal is a primary function. "How can you begin without knowing where you are going? With little if any sense of direction at the start, doesn't change risk moving the wrong way?" (Kotter and Cohen 2002, 23). Once the leader sees the way forward, he must inspire the people to come along for the journey. There are multiple means for doing this. Some have mastered the art of convincing people that they actually want to take a journey that is not the best for them. These leaders are actually masters at manipulation. They are using gullible people in an effort to accomplish their personal and selfish goals. I would suggest that another approach is best. "Transformational leadership is the process whereby a person engages with others and creates a connection that raises the level of motivation and morality in both the leader and the follower. This type of leader is attentive to the needs and motives of followers and tries to help followers reach their fullest potential" (Northouse 2010, 172). This is precisely what Moses has set out to do. He has seen the misery of his people and knows they long to be free in the land that God promised to their forefathers. He then, through God's inspiration at the burning bush, begins to see a way forward. He casts that vision, and now as the journey through the desert begins, he continually re-casts the same vision to remind the people of the compelling goals of freedom, self-determination, and a homeland. It is Moses' vision that is true, but it is also the desire and hope of the Israelites. When an inspired leader is placed in front of a motivated group of followers, miracles can ensue!

An Enduring Vision: Envision the future in such a way that people are willing to endure the journey to get there.

Inspiration only goes so far. The powerful inspiration of the halftime talk quickly wears off when the grinding and painful process of playing a grueling third quarter sets in. In Moses' case, the awe-inspiring moments of the plagues and the parting of the Red Sea fade quickly when tired feet and empty stomachs begin to set in. A vision must be more than simply compelling; it must be enduring. It helps that the Israelites have heard the stories of the Promised Land their entire lives. It helps that they have been longing for freedom and self-determination for their entire lives. However, there is still the drudgery of the process and danger of the journey. At this point, a leader needs more than beautiful, inspiring words. At this point, the vision must be played out in effective leadership, not simply beautiful speeches. "Followers need leaders able to effectively navigate for them. When they're facing life-and-death situations, the necessity is painfully obvious. But even when consequences aren't as serious, the need is also great. The truth is that nearly anyone can steer the ship, but it takes a leader to chart the course" (Maxwell 2007, 38). When their lives or careers are on the line, people must have confidence in the capacity of their leader to hear from God and clearly effect the change necessary to see them through the challenges of the journey. If that capacity to lead is lacking, the people will willingly desire to return to the relative safety of their enslavement.

A Worthy Vision: Envision the future in such a way that people are willing to fight for the ultimate prize.

In the end, the leader must be able to bring a final result. If it is a building program that is in front of the church, the pastor must be able to deliver a final, functional building. If it is relocation, the pastor must be able to bring the people to a piece of land that will become for them their promised land. Whatever the situation, organization, or context, the leader must be able to bring successful conclusion to the vision that he has presented. In order to do that, the leader must always be thinking and planning many steps ahead. Envisioning the final step and the battles that will be required to accomplish a given goal is imperative. We must be able to stand at the beginning and envision the end. "Being able to navigate for others requires a leader to possess a positive attitude. You've got to have faith that you can take your people all the way. If you can't confidently make the trip in your mind, you're not going to be able to take it in real life" (Maxwell 2007, 41).

Vision is the first of many keys in the development of an effective structure for any organization. Honestly, too many organizations, churches included, are simply structured to maintain the traditions of the past. They are built to function perfectly in our slavery. Once we have broken free from the bonds of the past, these old structures are no longer functional. New ways of doing things must be designed. New habits formed. New leadership teams and structures are required.

Those structures are not designed by our slave masters or within the context of our slavery. Those structures are designed in the awkward and sometimes frightening throes of radical and discontinuous change. They are designed with flexibility and mobility so that no matter what the road ahead may hold, the progress toward the compelling vision we have been given is enhanced, not entrapped. It's a new day, and now we must build a new system of leadership that can carry us where God is leading.

APPROPRIATELY EMPOWER LEADERS

But select capable men from all the people—men who fear God, trustworthy men who hate dishonest gain—and appoint them as officials over thousands, hundreds, fifties and tens. Have them serve as judges for the people at all times, but have them bring every difficult case to you; the simple cases they can decide themselves. That will make your load lighter, because they will share it with you. If you do this and God so commands, you will be able to stand the strain, and all these people will go home satisfied.

—*Exodus 18:21-23*

Creating a climate in which people are fully engaged and feel in control of their own lives is at the heart of strengthening others. Exemplary leaders build an environment that develops both people's abilities to perform a task and their self-confidence. In a climate of competence and confidence, people don't hesitate to hold themselves personally accountable for results, and they feel profound ownership for their achievements.

—James M. Kouzes and Barry Z. Posner
The Leadership Challenge

As we have already discussed, one of the first things I did upon arrival here in Southern Maryland to pastor New Life Church was to ask the volunteers if we could all act as staff even though I was not able to pay them. I wish I could say that I realized how important or how smart a move that was, but I didn't. Like so much in my life, the Holy Spirit just leads me to water and then waits for me to drink. Only later do I realize the miraculous nature of finding an oasis in this desert called leadership! When I began treating the volunteers as staff, they were empowered to lead in the areas of ministry I had assigned to them. They took that authority and self governed their actions in such a way that I did not need to hold accountability meetings or follow-up meetings to see that things were getting done. They simply understood that accomplishment of this particular goal was squarely in their realm of responsibility and no one else was going to get this thing done if they did not. As this culture of self-governance continued to take hold, the quality and quantity of what we were able to accomplish began to rise quickly. They became excited about the fact that God was using them. They started talking to everyone around them about their excitement and what God was doing. This attracted more people who held similar standards of self-governance, and then the process gained momentum. Driven people attracted driven people until the church began to grow at increasingly rapid rates. Building programs could not keep pace. We tried church planting and found that when we sent out a group with a church planter, another group as large or larger than the one sent out would show up at our services, sometimes the very week we sent out the new church! Right people who are properly empowered are the key to increased momentum.

Right People

While every pastor or leader will agree that right people make all the difference in the world, most will struggle to either find right people or recognize them when they arrive. The beauty of finding the right people (driven and self-governed) is that once you have found, empowered, and released them, they require very little management. "The right people don't need to be tightly managed or fired up; they will be self-motivated by the inner drive to produce the best results and to be part of creating something great" (Collins 2001, 42). Right people work hard and tend to do right things. Yes, they will mess up once in a while and leave you with something that must be cleaned up or set right. However, they do so with such pure motives that most of the time even the ones hurt by their wrong decisions are forgiving and understanding. The issue is finding right people. I may or may not help you here. Honestly, right people attract right people and wrong people attract wrong people. Said in a more acceptable way, leaders attract leaders and non-leaders attract non-leaders. If you are serving in a church filled with non-leaders (those who are not effectively self-managed or self-motivated), you will find it difficult to find, recruit, and retain people who are effectively self-managed and self-motivated. When true leaders enter into a culture that is lacking in leadership, they are quickly driven away. This occurs because the non-leadership culture is threatened by the leader and must get that threat out of its context, or the leader realizes he is not among peers. Either way, the result is the same. Like attracts like and deflects other. In order for you to find leaders, you must first become a leader yourself. Then you must motivate someone else, who is a leader, to stay with you and work at changing the culture. If you can retain one or two leaders, you can begin to change the overall culture of the organization or church you are leading.

There is a simple yet difficult truth here. When Moses set the new leadership structure for the new nation of Israel, he did not base it on the old elder structure that had been in place in Egypt. As was said earlier, there were likely deep and unforgiving mistrusts that had developed over decades between those who worked at making bricks and those who managed the making of bricks. So what Moses had to do was consider more than family ties and birth order. Moses had to consider competency.

Properly Empowered

As Moses sets the leadership structure that will carry these former slaves through the desert and ultimately transform them into a feared and respected nation, he does so not based on the old system of tribe and birth order. No doubt that the nation remained divided by tribe and birth order, as this was still a deep and meaningful way of organizing clans, but competency took the lead in consideration. Listen again to Jethro's advice: *"Select capable men from all the people—men who fear God, trustworthy men who hate dishonest gain—and appoint them as officials over thousands, hundreds, fifties and tens"* (Exodus 19:21). The key deciding factor in who would lead was based on who should lead, and not on who had always been leading or was next in line to lead. All too often in churches and organizations that lack a leadership culture, there is a tendency to lean on tribe and birth order considerations when appointing people to leadership positions. This tendency is understandable given the years of faithful service and commitment of these tribal elders. "How can you possibly choose to let some 'newbie' take the leadership role when Uncle John has been serving here so faithfully for the last 22 years?" Well, the answer is that the "newbie" has leadership skills and Uncle John does not. "But it just doesn't seem fair." What isn't fair is expecting Uncle John to do something he just doesn't have the capacity to do. People have different capacities. As we discussed earlier, there is no reason to believe that one set of capabilities is superior to another. This isn't a matter of good and better; it's just a matter of different. To ask someone to do what is beyond his or her capacity is not fair. "Leadership ability is always the lid on personal and organizational effectiveness. If a person's leadership is strong, the organization's lid is high. But if it's not, then the organization is limited" (Maxwell 2007, 7). When we ask people to perform or lead in areas that are beyond their lid or not even in their realm of understanding, we are not doing

227

them favors. Consider this perspective from Jim Collins in his book, *Good To Great*: "To let people languish in uncertainty for months or years, stealing precious time in their lives that they could use to move on to something else, when in the end they aren't going to make it anyway—*that* would be ruthless. To deal with it right up front and let people get on with their lives— that is rigorous" (Collins 2001, 53). While it may seem difficult or even cold for leadership to function this way, especially in church, it is the only fair and equitable way to actually choose a leadership team. Teams must be built with the right people, and those people must be properly empowered.

BUILD TEAMS

> *Moses listened to his father-in-law and did everything he said. He chose capable men from all Israel and made them leaders of the people, officials over thousands, hundreds, fifties and tens. They served as judges for the people at all times.*
>
> —*Exodus 18:24-26*

A powerful guiding group has two characteristics. It is made up of the right people, and it demonstrates teamwork. By the "right people," we mean individuals with the appropriate skills, the leadership capacity, the organizational credibility, and the connections to handle a specific kind of organizational change. We do not mean "good individuals" in any generic sense. Nor do we necessarily mean the existing senior management committee.

—John P. Kotter and Dan S. Cohen
The Heart of Change

Recently I had a pastor come and ask me about the difference between church leadership at different levels of growth and church size. In my perspective, leadership changes happen at some key growth points. Now, I am going to set some arbitrary size numbers here. While there is research establishing some of these size levels, the real changes happen at key points of limitations for the leader, not the organization. When the leader hits his lid of leadership, something must change. Either the leader must grow beyond his current lid, or the organization must expand to accommodate growth beyond the leader. In most cases, leaders learn to grow themselves in order to go to the next level of leadership. This is the most common choice because it is the easiest choice. The leader, in order to become a leader, has already been working to build self-discipline and self-improvement into his life. Therefore, it is just not that great a stretch to increase those levels of personal development in order to go to another level. While every leader should be doing this work of constantly improving his leadership capacity, there are limitations to the effectiveness of this approach. In the end, the organization is still limited by the leader's capacity, albeit an increased or significant capacity. This leaves the organization with marginal growth potential and limited reach. If the organization can change, then perhaps it can grow beyond the capacity of the leader.

It didn't take me long as a pastor to reach my lid. We have already discussed the fact that I view myself as a 150 guy. I can effectively lead 150 people. Now, having reached 150, I am left with two choices.

1. Expand my personal leadership capacity

If I should choose to take this route of expanding my personal leadership capacity within the given organizational structure, I will see gains. I may be able to double or even triple my leadership lid and expand what I am able to do by tremendous amounts. This will take Herculean efforts and deep levels of commitment and self-discipline to accomplish. When it is all said and done, I will lead an organization of 300 or 450 people. This is impressive by any standard, but more is possible.

2. Export authority to other leaders

I could also choose to export authority to other leaders. If I should choose this route of expanding my organization's leadership capacity, then the potential for growth far outstrips the 300 to 450 capacity set in my personal leadership. Exporting authority to other leaders allows for more than incremental growth. It allows for exponential growth. Therefore, the real power of the organization will be limited as long I insist on being the only avenue through which the organization can grow. However, if I am willing to allow the organization to grow beyond my abilities, capacities, and, in some cases, control, the potential for growth then becomes virtually unlimited.

In the end, here is how I answered that pastor who asked me about leadership in different size congregations.

0-300: Relational Capacity

From, let's say, 0 to 300 in attendance, the responsibility of gathering people and growing the church is completely dependent on the ability of the lead pastor to find and keep new church members. Everyone in the church has some type of relationship to that pastor. Everyone in the church views that communicating lead pastor as his or her spiritual shepherd. At this point, all the weight of leading, managing, caring, comforting, and communicating the vision falls squarely on the shoulders of that one leader. Now, everyone has a different lid for this type of leadership. Some can accomplish this with no more than 30 folks while others could potentially reach up toward 300. I have already stated that I fall in the 150-range. I choose 300 as the limiting factor for this based solely on my life experience. I have simply never seen anyone lead past 300 in this type of leadership scenario. Let me be completely honest about a weakness in this leadership scenario. It is exhausting! This is the most common form of leadership structure within churches today. A lead pastor who does all or the vast majority of the communicating, counseling, recruiting, caring, marrying, burying, baby-dedicating, loving, and recruiting of the people. Is it any wonder that burnout is so common among pastors? John Maxwell got this right when he said, "If you do everything alone and never partner with other people, you create huge barriers to your own potential" (Maxwell 2001, 8). If I may borrow a phrase from Jethro, *"What you are doing is not good."*

300 - 1,500: Organizational Capacity

Now, once a congregation surpasses the leadership lid of the pastor there are only two options. Either the organization will change in structure to accommodate growth beyond the abilities of the pastor, or the congregation will shrink to meet the abilities of the pastor. Some pastors would prefer the congregation shrink to accommodate their abilities. These pastors would rather not grow than give authority or adoration away. "In a culture that sings the praises of individual gold medals and where a person fights for rights instead of focusing on taking responsibility, people tend to lose sight of the big picture. In fact, some people seem to believe that they *are* the entire picture" (Maxwell 2001, 17). The actual truth is that we must create teams in order to move beyond our own personal limitations. Consider this statement from the book, *Built To Last*: "Visionary companies require great and charismatic visionary leaders. A charismatic visionary leader is absolutely *not required* for visionary company and, in fact, can be detrimental to a company's long-term prospects" (Collins and Porras 2002, 7). In other words, a person with a lower lid, say 150 instead of 300, can achieve at a very high level if that person is willing to build the team necessary to take the organization to the next level. Teams can succeed at increasingly high levels if multiple leaders are all pulling the same direction at one time. Therefore, it stands to reason that more can be accomplished through a number of teams than can be accomplished through a single leader.

1,500 and Beyond: Systematic Capacity

Just as there are limits to the potential of a single leader, there are limits to the potential capacity of a single set of teams. One can only produce so many "widgets" in one factory. However, if a company that produces "widgets" in a single factory in, let's say, Charlotte, North Carolina, reaches its optimal output capacity, that does not mean that the company is done. Another plant, duplicating the same processes, ideas, leadership structure, and production mentality can be established in, let's say, Richmond, Virginia. Now, that plant can duplicate the efforts of the plant in Charlotte without causing the inevitable log jam of leaders when all of these processes are jammed into one space. This is a matter of building systems that can be exported to other locations and implemented with similar results. This creates a layered effect. I suppose the first time I ever noticed this was when I was growing up just outside of Kannapolis, North Carolina. This small suburb of Charlotte, North Carolina was known for one thing, Cannon Mills. Back in the day, Cannon Mills produced some of the best textiles in the country. Growing up, both my family and my wife's family had multiple members that worked at Cannon Mills. All of the production of this company was not held in one location. There were multiple plants in Kannapolis, where the corporate headquarters was located, but there were also plants in all of the surrounding towns. Each plant operated in a very similar, and sometimes identical, fashion. Each plant produced somewhat similar and sometimes identical products. Each plant was striving to operate at its optimal level of productivity. This allowed the company to avoid log jams of leadership in a single plant. Instead, they identified what they found to be the optimal size for production and profitability, and then they built multiple layers of that model in different locations. In doing so, they maximized the productivity of each plant and learned from the best practices of each plant manager. If one plant were outperforming the other, they would go and see what was different there and apply this new way of doing things to the other places. This layering allowed for increased productivity, improved quality, and maximum profitability.

Now, I don't run a textile plant. I pastor a church. If we really think about it, there are some correlations here. Moses, as he organized the people of Israel, chose leaders based on their capacity: *"officials over thousands, hundreds, fifties and tens."* He did not do away with the tribal nature that had been so ingrained in the people from the time of Jacob. Choose from all the people. Instead, he layered the teamwork structure within each tribe in order to achieve unity in structure while maintaining uniqueness in tribe. This same system is doable within the church world.

When energy outstrips capacity

If an organization continually grows for a long period of time, there will come a point when the energy of the organization outstrips the capacity of the organization at some level. With Moses, we see this outstripping of capacity with the long, exhausting lines of people attempting to get guidance from one man, Moses. In Cannon Mills, we see it in the limitations of one plant in one place to efficiently produce the volume of textiles needed. In churches, we see it in the leadership capacity of the pastor, or in the seating capacity of the church building. Over the years, the answer for churches has been to build even bigger buildings and larger staffing to accommodate the energy of an increased congregation. While this practice is not, in and of itself, bad, it is limited. Eventually, the larger congregations begin to see diminished output from a given number of individual members or attenders. They find themselves facing a log jam of leaders within this one large congregation. People begin to look around at the overwhelming number of others in the room and assume that their talents and abilities are really not needed. At this point, they simply sit and soak in the congregation failing to use the gifts and abilities given to them by God, or they leave and find somewhere that needs them. This reduces the overall productivity of the congregation in the work of spreading the gospel. In order to overcome this dilemma, the most common practices have been increased levels of discipleship in an effort to close the back door of the church. However, even this has been practiced with limited success.

What if we tried something different? What if we layered the efforts by launching new churches using the leadership, structure, philosophy, and patterns of the healthy congregation to start new congregations? What if we did this in a more localized sense than has traditionally been done in the past? What if, instead of New Life Church in La Plata, Maryland, solely planting churches in other states, we choose to plant churches just a few miles up the road? When we do this, we can take advantage of the Cannon Mills model. When launching a church in another state, the mother church must send a leader who must then find, recruit, train, and deploy leaders in ministry. The mother church must then simply trust that the leader they sent will impart the proper vision and values into the new leaders and congregation. However, when a church is planted just up the street, something different happens. Something powerful.

With the measure you use

In the Gospel of Luke, Jesus makes a promise to us. *"Give, and it will be given to you. A good measure, pressed down, shaken together and running over, will be poured into your lap. For with the measure you use, it will be measured to you"* (Luke 6:38). This promise is often preached about in churches across the world. I have heard sermons on this many times. Virtually, every time I have heard a sermon on this passage, it has been about giving money to the church. I can remember so many times hearing the pastor implore the people convincing them that if they give money to the ministry then God will bless them *"a good measure, pressed down, shaken together and running over."* Those same pastors refuse to even consider giving away tithing parishioners for the start

237

of another church down the street. That seems wrong to them. It seems divisive. It seems like a loss. However, we must change our perspective. Just like Moses, we cannot continue to hoard the blessings of ministry and leadership to ourselves. Pastors must change their perspective. "All too often, leaders fail to realize the importance of sharing power and delegating authority to others. They don't understand that by empowering others, they themselves will gain. And even if they understand this in the abstract, they do not take the next step to establish criteria for delegating authority" (Cohen 2007, 95).

If it is true (and I believe that it is) that God will return to us His blessing for our generosity, then this truth cannot be limited to money. It must also be true that when we give away people, leaders, and tithers, God will miraculously replace them with *"a good measure, pressed down, shaken together and running over."* Can we trust Him to do so? Here's a better question: Will we trust Him to do so? God is always true to His promises. Although, I realize that it can be tough to trust God when giving away the very source of your personal and financial security, God always makes it worthwhile. One of my mentors, Wayne Schmidt, in recalling the moment he actually had to follow through with letting go of leaders in order to plant a church, perfectly captures the internal struggle of a sending pastor:

> Did I truly believe the he is Jehovah Jireh, our Provider? Would I place my treasure—which I then measured in terms of staff members, attendees, and financial

resources—in God's hands? Or would I keep them tightly under my control? Would my ministry, and my personal life, be characterized by generosity thinking or by a scarcity mind-set? (Schmidt 2017, 82)

These are very real struggles. There are no guarantees. It may be that God will gain glory for Himself by blessing you far beyond your expectations — *"a good measure, pressed down, shaken together and running over."* It may be that God will gain glory for Himself by blessing you with the faith to learn to trust Him in a time of struggle. Either way, you must trust the God who provides. In our story here at New Life, we have seen God provide in miraculous ways as we have stepped out in faith to plant churches. When we plant locally, we have never failed to see God return every dime of investment back to the sending church within the first year of ministry. When we plant locally, we have never seen a dip in our attendance or volunteerism. In fact, we have seen moments where we sent out 250 only to have God send back 350 on the same Sunday. It has been amazing to watch, but that is a matter of God's math.

As leaders in God's Kingdom, we must realize that greatness requires more than just me. John Maxwell says it this way, "That's why I assert that *one is too small a number to achieve greatness.* You cannot do anything of *real* value alone. That is the Law of Significance" (Maxwell 2001, 4). So at whatever level you are leading or to whatever level you are transitioning, you must involve others. Whether you are simply working to expand the output of your team, working to establish church growth teams, or you are working to establish church launch teams, you must always remember this: "We gain power not to enrich ourselves by creating a power base, but in order to share it appropriately with others" (Schmidt 2006, 125). In doing so, God will add to our lives and our ministry, *"a good measure, pressed down, shaken together and running over."*

EXCELLENCE TAKES TIME

> *On the first day of the third month after the Israelites left Egypt—on that very day—they came to the Desert of Sinai.*
>
> *—Exodus 19:1*

What Moses models is more than leadership methods or techniques — he models his own transformation even as he aims to transform the people. What Moses experiences in his own self becomes the mirror through which he will learn to understand the people and reach out to them as he tries to elevate them. He will learn to connect with them while never sacrificing his ability or desire to speak with God "face to face." Moses, as a transformational leader, must first and foremost transform himself.

—Zvi Grumet, *Moses and the Path to Leadership*

At the beginning of Exodus, chapter 19, the people of Israel arrive at Mount Sinai. They will remain here all the way through chapter 31. This is a time period of about one full year. While that may not seem like a long time to you, it must have seemed like forever for a group of former slaves now living out of tents in a desert place that is not going to be their final destination. God has the nation pause here at Mount Sinai, so that he can give Moses the instructions that will be necessary for them moving forward. Here at Sinai, the actual rules that will govern life as an Israelite are born. As Moses ascends the mountain to speak with God, the nation is left in the hands of Aaron. Although it seems that he is there a long time, it is imperative that Moses gets this year right. In this year, God will reveal how the Israelites are to handle their own personal lives through the 10 commandments (Exodus 20), deal with servants and personal injuries (Exodus 21), protection of property and social responsibility (Exodus 22), justice, mercy, festivals, and spiritual guidance (Exodus 23), the covenant of God (Exodus 24), and the worship of God through the Tabernacle, altars, and the priesthood (Exodus 25-31). All of these instructions will prove central to the functioning of a well-structured and peaceful society. As we mentioned, Moses has led a group of slaves, who have never run a nation, into a desert that can scarcely sustain its own wildlife. There must be rules and direction in order to maintain balance and peace.

It is here at Mount Sinai that the intricacies of Jewish law begin to take form. The detailed descriptions of worship, living, and dealing with oneself and one's neighbor are given to Moses first here at Sinai. These laws and decrees will serve the people well as a guide to godliness and holiness. Jesus, as He so masterfully does, sums them all up in just a few sentences: " *'Love the Lord your God with all your heart and with all your soul and with all your mind.' This is the first and greatest commandment. And the second is like it: 'Love you neighbor as yourself.' All the Law and the Prophets hang on these two commandments"* (Matthew 22:37-40). One might wonder why God didn't simply give Moses those few sentences uttered by Jesus? The answer is one of context. God needed to change the very culture of the Israelites in order to completely remove them from the slavery mindset they had developed in Egypt. There, under the rule of the Egyptians, they had been taught a concept of god that was not in keeping with the God of Heaven. The God of the Israelites was not the same as the gods of the Egyptians. The God of Israel wanted a specific set of rules, actions, and reactions from His people. He required holiness and not just might. He required compassion and not just shrewdness. He required the Israelites to understand Him as one God, not a multiplicity of deities that are fighting for position. God was their God, and the society He would require of them was dramatically different than the one they had left. Changing that mindset would require work, and making it stick would require time. It was absolutely imperative to the future of Israel that these changes were made.

> Tradition is a powerful force. Leaps into the future can slide back into the past. We keep a change in place by helping to create a new, supportive, and sufficiently strong organizational culture. A supportive culture provides roots for the new ways of operating. It keeps the revolutionary technology, the globalized organization, the innovative strategy, or the more efficient processes working to make you a winner. (Kotter and Cohen 2002, 159).

As pastors, we often need to change the culture of our churches. These changes can be difficult to achieve. However, we often neglect the work of making those changes stick by failing to enact very real patterns and structures that constantly remind our people of the new way of doing things. When I was pastoring in North Carolina, I served at a wonderful church in a mid-sized town. I was the pastor there for more than six years. During that time, we made great strides toward renewal and culture change, but there was one accomplishment I did not achieve. The congregation wanted to build an expansion onto the existing structure. I drew plans and thought through strategies to get this project completed. I worked to move forward with their stated goal. While all of this planning was going on, we paved a new parking lot. I knew that once the new building was built there would be a parking area off to the side running the length of the building. So when we built our parking lot, I had them build a long narrow parking area that jutted far back into the empty yard. It was odd looking. This random parking area stuck way back into an empty lot with acres of grass sitting where it seemed the pavement should have been. Yes, I could have simply built a deeper parking area that didn't stick out like that, but I was building a reminder. I wanted that weird parking lot to constantly remind the people of the church that a building belonged here. I wanted them to park in the back, and as they took the long walk to the existing building envision the new structure that would sit on all that undisturbed grass. I wanted to set a mindset that would stick. Now, I don't believe they ever built that building. I guarantee you they often have to answer the question of why the parking lot is designed so weirdly. Every time, they have to recall the building that was supposed to go there. Only once that building is in place will the pavement make sense. It stands as a constant reminder of what was supposed to be next.

These types of reminders must be designed well and implemented consistently over time. This implementation will require enforcement. Honestly, some will view our enforcement of a new cultural expectation as an overreach or as simple ruthlessness on the part of the leader. However, we must understand that rigorous enforcement of agreed-upon, Spirit-led cultural change is not ruthless; it is actually loving, and it is required to make cultural change last. Jim Collins gives some insight to this in his book, *Good To Great*:

> To be ruthless means hacking and cutting, especially in difficult times, or wantonly firing people without any thoughtful consideration. To be rigorous means consistently applying exacting standards at all times and at all levels, especially in upper management. To be rigorous, not ruthless, means that the best people need not worry about their positions and can concentrate fully on their work. (Collins 2001, 52)

A rigorous enforcement of the new cultural norm is required in order to drive the cultural change deep within the psyche of the organization. Without this work, the change just won't stick. When we take the time to do it right, we build thinking and culture that remains over the long haul.

Remember, what you are establishing today is the tradition that will govern tomorrow. If you take the time to design it right, it will be the tradition of multiple generations. There are no shortcuts to this kind of culture change. It takes tons of time on the mountain hearing from God. It can take a generation of reminding and leading the people. It takes the tenacity to never give up. Excellence, in any and every area of life and leadership, takes time. It is time well spent.

5

LEARNING TO LEAVE A MOVEMENT

> *When the whole nation had finished crossing the Jordan, the LORD said to Joshua, "Choose twelve men from among the people, one from each tribe, and tell them to take up twelve stones from the middle of the Jordan, from right where the priests are standing, and carry them over with you and put them down at the place where you stay tonight."*
>
> *—Joshua 4:1-3*

Before we move on we should clarify what a movement is. In a general sense, movements are informal groupings of people and organizations pursuing a common cause. They are people with an agenda for change. Movements don't have members, but they do have participants. The goals of a movement can be furthered by organizations, but organizations are not the totality of a movement. A movement can have leading figures, but no one person or group controls a movement. Movements are made up of people committed to a common cause.

—Steve Addison
Movements That Change The World

Let me be clear. I intend to grow the church I pastor to the greatest degree possible.

I make that statement in order to avoid any high-minded idea of nobility within the mind of the reader as we discuss this final portion of our look into the life of Moses. I intend to grow the church in the same way that Moses intended to lead the Israelites into the Promised Land. He intended to build the structure and social norms that would sustain them and build them into a nation that would be strong, stable, respected, and godly. Moses intended to lead them into the Promised Land. Though he did not get to actually cross the Jordan River with them, he did bring them right to the edge. God allowed Moses to look over to the land from a pinnacle of Mount Nebo (Deuteronomy 34). I wonder, as Moses looked over the river to this Promised Land where he had never set foot, what were his thoughts? What did he actually see? He certainly could not imagine the majesty and splendor of the reigns of King David and King Solomon. He could likely not have borne the tragedy of a divided nation and the ultimate fall of both Israel and Judah. He would have been crushed at the return to slavery that the Israelites faced for centuries. One can only be grateful that he did not have to witness the ultimate fall of Jerusalem in 70 A.D., and it is only God's grace that could have spared him the horror of the Holocaust. But then, how could anyone have imagined the return of a nation, a language, and a people that had been dispersed for centuries in the 1948 re-emergence of Israel? What a tumultuous and tremendous journey.

All of this is what happens in a movement. We view movements in a single set of years or a single generation of time. In reality, as Christians, we are all part of a massive movement that has been going on for more than 2,000 years. "Jesus was the first missionary. He didn't start an organization, he didn't write a book, and he didn't run for office. What Jesus did was to found a missionary movement that would one day span the globe" (Addison 2011, 29). Today, we are still part of that movement. Honestly, the movement has been challenged by more enemies than one could imagine, many from outside and even more from within.

But the movement continues.

Schisms, splits, and battles over theology, orthodoxy, and doctrine have resulted in so many denominations and organizations that it would be difficult, if not impossible, to number them all. Cultural challenges and governmental decrees have limited, persecuted, or outlawed the church.

But the movement continues.

Kings and nations have come and gone. Dynasties and dictators have risen and fallen. Ideas and cultures have flourished and died. Philosophies have claimed absolute truth only to fade away into obscurity. Technology has expanded and knowledge has increased. Wars have raged and evil has flourished.

But the movement continues.

Churches and denominations have attempted to manufacture revival and fake movements. Some still call themselves movements, even when there has been no movement in that movement in decades. All the while, the gospel of Christ is preached.

And the movement continues.

I am part of a denominational church. I am part of a tribe of Christians called the Wesleyans. My family has been part of this tribe for more than 100 years. I must face a simple reality. The Wesleyans are not a movement, at least not at the moment. We are an organization. Organizations are specifically designed to contain movement. Said another way, organizations kill movements by structuring them and holding them captive. All of this is well intentioned. We begin organizations to standardize the energy and power that comes out of a movement. We want to make certain that pastors are properly trained and given proper oversight. We want to make sure that theology is properly protected and defended from heresy and abuse. We desire to ensure that funds are properly managed and people are in good care. All of this is good, but it isn't indicative of a true movement. I am not opposed to any of these organizational realities. I am actually uncomfortable with independent churches and leaders who seem (to me) to have little to no accountability in their ministry. My comfort within this organization that I love does nothing to negate the fact that the organization itself fights against the formation of a movement.

The truth is that I really desire to see a movement of God among the people of this world in this day. My heart yearns for this. At the core of my being, I don't care if they are Wesleyan, Baptist, Catholic, Orthodox, Independent, or Pentecostal. I just want them to know Jesus, the original missionary. He is the ultimate answer. He is the ultimate hope. So the question of this section (honestly, I pray the question that animates the remainder of my life) is how do we, as established leaders, foster a movement that can endure thousands of years of persecution and power? How do we, like Moses, go to our graves knowing that we have, at the very least, brought our people to the edge of greatness? How do we count on God to once again part waters to make way for the next great movement of His will and His power? Oh, God, help us to set the stage and get out of Your way!

And the movement continues.

KEEP GOD IN THE CENTER OF EVERYTHING

> *The LORD said to Moses, "Tell the Israelites to bring me an offering. You are to receive the offering for me from everyone whose heart prompts him to give. These are the offerings you are to receive from them: gold, silver and bronze; blue, purple and scarlet yarn and fine linen; goat hair; ram skins dyed red and another type of durable leather; acacia wood; olive oil for the light; spices for the anointing oil and for the fragrant incense; and onyx stones and other gems to be mounted on the ephod and breastpiece. Then have them make a sanctuary for me, and I will dwell among them. Make this tabernacle and all its furnishings exactly like the pattern I will show you."*
>
> *—Exodus 25:1-9*

There is a third goal leaders should have for their organizations, one which is the ultimate goal of any organization and the reason behind the first two goals of leadership—to bring God glory. Whether people lead Christian or secular organizations, their goal ought to be to glorify God by the way they lead their organization.

—Henry and Richard Blackaby, *Spiritual Leadership*

As God describes to Moses how to take the offering and make the plans for the construction of a Tabernacle for the presence of God, He sets the stage for a visible lesson that will stand true for the Israelites for thousands of years. He will design this dwelling place for God using the best and finest of all the gifts the people bring together and will place it squarely in the center of the people. Whenever the nation of Israel sets up camp, the Tabernacle will establish the center of the encampment. Whenever the nation of Israel sets out to travel forward, the Tabernacle will serve as their guide and will establish the order in which they travel (Numbers 2).

From the very beginning of the nation, Moses visibly establishes God as the very center of their existence. Unfortunately, this centrality of God is lost on modern culture. It is interesting to consider that most people don't see God as being at the front of their priority list, or even at the front of their week. In the U.S. context, we still tend to worship on Sunday. Sunday is the first day of the week and the day on which Jesus rose from the dead. His resurrection is literally an indication of a new beginning. Therefore, the church has worshipped on the morning of the first day of the week for centuries now. However, most of us do not view it that way any longer. In reality, we view Sunday, not as the beginning of the week, but as the end of the weekend. Therefore, God is figuratively placed at the end of the end, not at the beginning of the beginning. God is not understood to be central in our lives, at least not any longer. There was a day in our culture where God was, at least figuratively, at the center. Travel to almost any old east coast town and you will find at the very center of the town a few buildings. There will be a town hall of some sort, usually a courthouse, often an open central grassy area for town gatherings, and right there in the center of it all, will be an old church. Often, this downtown church is one of the oldest buildings in town and has been long since protected by some historical society. It is there for a reason. As these towns were established, the people building them understood from the Old Testament and Moses that the dwelling place of God should be in the center of community life. The church should be in the center of the town. It shouldn't be competing with city hall or railing against the courthouse. It should be standing next to and in harmony with both. Nation and God standing together for a people who need both. But those days are lost. No amount of nostalgia could or even should bring them back.

In our modern culture, we must take a much different and often a far more individualistic approach to keeping God at the center of our existence. The issue is not how one keeps God at the center; the issue is that one keeps God at the center. True spirituality is essential among leaders, and especially among pastoral leaders.

As the "shepherd of a flock," the pastor has an important responsibility for the spiritual development of the people in the church. Even though this responsibility is great, a far greater responsibility is the spiritual development of himself or herself. If the pastor does

> not have a growing, vibrant, dynamic relationship
> with God, then how can he or she successfully lead
> others in their spiritual development? If the pastor's
> spiritual development is weak, everyone will suffer the
> consequences. (Petersen et al. 2010, 240)

God must remain at the very center of our thinking, planning, actions, and thoughts. Otherwise, we are not building His Kingdom; we are simply building ours.

Keeping God at the center of all our leadership and planning is not a simple task. As leaders, we learn patterns and techniques to more effectively lead our people to the places we know God wants them to go. As we apply those patterns and techniques, we can get into such an effective rhythm that we forget it is the presence and power of the Holy Spirit that enables all that we do. We can become so good at what we do that we fail to remember that it is God who makes what we do good. Go back with me for a moment to the town square in all those little old towns. Most often, when the towns were first established, it was clear to the people establishing the town that the church was absolutely necessary in the center of their community. That was the building that was most important and most needed. However, through decades of good leadership and practice, the town hall became the most necessary building. Today, government is so pervasive and necessary in our daily lives that it is not difficult to believe that we need the government more than we need God. In fact, entire systems of thought are built around that exact premise.

In the beginning of our nation, we passed laws out of a fear that the government (from its second chair position in society) would violate the church (in its first chair position in society). Today, that trend is reversed. It is reversed because in our daily practice, it is government that sits in the first chair. God has been demoted. While the church building still stands at the end of the town square, very few ever enter it. But the town hall and courthouse … well, everybody has to go in there at some point. Now, I am not speaking against effective government or even fairly pervasive government. I am proud of our culture and society and the way our governmental agencies attempt to work for the people of our nation. However, that does not negate the fact that God has been demoted in our culture. As pastoral leaders, we honestly hold little power to change the nature and work of government in our current culture. We must remain vigilant, lest the altar of God in our churches be demoted to second chair, behind the pastor's office.

YOU CAN'T STAY ON THE MOUNTAIN AND LEAD

> *Then the LORD said to Moses, "Go down, because your people, whom you brought up out of Egypt, have become corrupt."*
>
> —*Exodus 32:7*

Moses spends forty days on Mount Sinai in the Divine Presence, receiving God's laws, which he will subsequently convey to the People of Israel. The grandeur of this encounter stands in sharp contrast to the feelings of abandonment that the Israelites experience at the foot of the mountain, bereft of their leader.

—Norman J. Cohen
Moses and the Journey to Leadership

Often, people fail to remember that it is God who is awesome, not us. As a norm, humans have a tendency to become self-centered and self-focused. When this happens, we tend to believe that we have the best ideas and God becomes little more than a good luck charm that we wish on. The God of Heaven is not a good luck charm. The God of Heaven is not a wishing well. The God of Heaven is the all-powerful Creator, and we do not have to wish for His involvement in this world; we can depend on it. Leaders must carefully, consistently, and sometimes forcefully do the work of communicating the greatness of God to their people. This issue came front and center for Moses very quickly.

Failure of Perspective

"When the people saw that Moses was so long in coming down from the mountain, they gathered around Aaron and said, 'Come, make us gods who will go before us. As for this fellow Moses who brought us up out of Egypt, we don't know what has happened to him.'" (Exodus 32:1)

Moses spends forty days on the mountain with God. While he was there experiencing firsthand the greatness of God on a daily basis, the people were confused and worried. Leaders, especially pastors, need desperately to understand that just because you are experiencing the greatness and goodness of God does not mean that your people are seeing and feeling the same thing. While you are on a mountaintop meeting with God, they are in the valley working. They are focused on the mundane and monotonous task of survival. They are not seeing all the miracles you see or hearing the voice of God that you hear. They can become confused and concerned at this seeming absence of their leader and their God. When that happens, they will resort to the comfort of old ways and bad habits. They will reach out to the good luck charms of their past while living within walking distance of the very presence of God. In their fear and insecurity, they will sit beneath the cloud of God's presence and set up powerless "gods" in the form of addictions, work, wealth, relationships, and the like. They will begin to worship everything but the God of Heaven. Part of the failure can be yours. If you don't regularly communicate to your people the power and goodness of God, they will forget why they are doing what they are doing. They will forget who brought them out of slavery, and they will actually return to the practices that you helped deliver them from. You must carefully and constantly remind people of the greatness of our God. You must do the work of seeing life and ministry through the eyes of your people. You are living this ministry and this presence of God thing every day. They are not. They are working and surviving. They are simply focused on keeping food on the table, clothes on the kids, and electricity in the house. You may have wonderful times with the Lord on your Mount Sinai (the worship center of the church you work in), but they don't experience that. Somehow, you must do the work of showing them and helping them see the greatness of the God you have the privilege of meeting with and working for every day.

Failure of Practice

"When Aaron saw this [a golden calf idol], he built an altar in front of the calf and announced, 'Tomorrow there will be a festival to the LORD.'" (Exodus 32:5)

Not only must you carefully and constantly remind the people of the centrality and greatness of God, you must do the same work with your leadership team and staff. Just like the rest of the people, they are not on the mountaintop with you. They do not experience the calling and leading of the Holy Spirit with you and therefore can get confused as to what should be the next move. In the absence of guidance from the leader, even other leaders can fall back to old ways. Political and social pressures can drive leaders into patterns of failure and back into patterns of bondage. Sometimes the pressure from people can lead other leaders astray. You may think that Aaron has personally lost faith when he builds the golden calf, but Cohen gives some interesting insight here:

> According to the predominant rabbinic tradition, this is not the reason why Aaron builds the calf. Angered and dismayed at Moses's protracted stay on the mountain, the people first approach the elders, those who are closer to them, and request a leader. Because the elders rebuke the people for provoking the Divine after witnessing all the miracles God has wrought, the people kill them. They then turn to Hur, Miriam's son and Moses's nephew, with the same request. Hur also courageously refuses even though he would meet the same fate. (Cohen 2007, 112)

Aaron caves to the threatening attitude of the people and gives them the idolatrous symbol of Egyptian leadership they're looking for in the absence of Moses. Moses would never have allowed such a thing, but Aaron is not as strong. You simply cannot assume that they understand the power of what God is doing in and through your life just because you hired them, trained them, spoke with them yesterday or last week, or are even related to them. It's not that your experience with God is any more significant than anyone else's experience. It's just that God has called you to be the leader and to do so through your experience with Him. The purity and centrality of the greatness of God must be protected and announced. Even after you have brought your people so far and accomplished so much, especially after much achievement, you must defend even more vigorously the centrality and greatness of God.

> Moses the zealot successfully completes his mission. As God's emissary, he frees the Israelites from their slavery, humbles Pharaoh, demonstrates the uniqueness of God, brings the people to Mount Sinai, and brokers the Giving of the Torah. His zealotry for his people and for the human condition is unleashed and knows no bounds, until those very people betray Moses's partner. Moses remains the zealot, but the object of his passion shifts from the people to God. (Grumet 2014, 46)

Failure of Deflected Praise

Years and decades of effective leadership is the goal of every leader and every pastor. If we are not careful those decades of effectiveness will turn in to an idol all its own. These people who have followed Moses out of Egypt are not dismissing his importance or forgetting his leadership. They are afraid he is dead. In his absence, they need to find direction and protection. They know and trust Moses. They do not know this God who Moses speaks of and therefore is afraid. In the same way, the people who are following you are slowly learning to depend on you. If you are not careful, they will learn to depend on you more than God. Even while His presence looms over the mountains in ominous cloud and lightning, they will resort to a powerless god who they can see, touch, handle, and control. You have become for them the physical manifestation of the presence of God. While this is a great responsibility and blessing, it also comes fraught with great danger.

> Moses has become too much of a focus of power and authority. It is he who brought them out of Egypt, divided the waters of the Red Sea, and miraculously provided them with sustenance in the desert. Their idolatry, so to speak, begins long before the building of the Golden Calf—Moses himself has become an object of reverence for them, upon whom they are pathologically dependent. (Cohen 2007, 111)

You must over-communicate the centrality and greatness of God in order for your people to see that the power is from God and not you. If you don't, the ministry you have given your life to build could become a little more than a golden calf in the desert.

YOU CAN'T LEAD THOSE YOU DON'T LOVE

> *"I have seen these people," the LORD said to Moses, "and they are a stiff-necked people. Now leave me alone so that my anger may burn against them and that I may destroy them. Then I will make you into a great nation." But Moses sought the favor of the LORD his God, "LORD," he said, "why should your anger burn against your people, whom you brought out of Egypt with great power and a mighty hand?"*
>
> —*Exodus 32:9-11*

In recent times, upheavals in society have energized a tremendous demand for authentic leadership. The destruction on 9/11, corporate scandals at companies like WorldCom and Enron, and massive failures in the banking industry have all created fear and uncertainty. People feel apprehensive and insecure about what is going on around them, and, as a result, they long for bona fide leadership they can trust and for leaders who are honest and good.

—Peter G. Northouse
Leadership Theory and Practice

What Peter Northouse calls "authentic leadership," I would like to describe as love. Now, you will rarely find this word in leadership texts and journals. The idea of love as a trait of leadership feels soft and mushy. The concept in the arena of pastoral leadership is central and foundational. People must know that the pastor loves them before they will ever take the risk of letting the pastor lead them. The simple fact is that no one has to go to church. Church is truly a free-market system and is perhaps one of the few, true free-market systems left in our culture. People can choose every week whether or not they wish to darken the doors of a church. Most, if we are to be honest, choose not to come. One of the reasons people have given up on church is that the leadership inside these churches seems inauthentic. Leaders are more worried about budgets and programs than they are about people and society. It can often seem that the politicians and governmental agencies care more about real people than the pastors and churches. Far too often, pastors have learned so much about leadership from a secular point of view that they have forgotten to see leadership from a biblical point of view. Now, let's be honest. Effective leadership requires some cold, hard facts and some cold, hard decisions. However, that need for harsh realism does not negate the possibility of real love for the people you lead. Moses is a wonderful example of this. He was effective and powerful in the way he led the nation of Israel. He was decisive and (at times) made cold, hard choices that could cause the most callous of leaders to cringe. Yet Moses, one of the greatest leaders in human history, did not fail to love his people. He desired what was best for them, even when it was directly opposed to what might have been best for him.

Serve People

"Servant leadership is an approach to guiding the church that is well suited for the twenty-first century. It is not a technique as much as an attitude or spiritual commitment, based on biblical principles, to humbly serve those who are being led" (Petersen et al. 2010, 197). The role of the pastor, ultimately, is the role of a servant. Whether through teaching biblical truth, enacting effective leadership practices and patterns, shepherding people through hazardous times, or celebrating with people during wonderful events, the work of the pastor is the work of being a servant. When I am officiating a wedding, I have a phrase that I always use during the rehearsal. Addressing the entire wedding party, I set the following guidelines for the wedding ceremony. "From the back of the church to the stage, do everything the wedding director tells you to do. From the stage to the end of the ceremony, do everything I tell you to do. And once this is over (look at the groom), you do everything she tells you to do!" That last sentence always gets a good laugh. I will then point out, "My goal here is that tomorrow you can simply enjoy the wedding. You won't have to even think. We will do that for you." This is not a control trip that I am taking with the wedding director. This is servanthood. I am not attending this wedding for the purpose of enjoyment. Although, these days, I officiate very few weddings and generally have a very close relationship to the couple or their family, so they are always enjoyable. I am attending this wedding to serve. I serve as the leader. I serve as the officiant. I serve as the one who will declare God's blessing and recognition of this union. I serve as the authorizing official on behalf of the government. I serve a lot of roles when I officiate a wedding, but the one constant is that I serve. Pastors must be capable of serving. I actually find myself slightly nauseous when I encounter one of those pastors who are kings in their congregation. Everyone running around trying to serve that one man and elevate him. I just can't figure that out. The role of pastor itself sets us apart. There is no reason for my parking space to further that separation. Perhaps, as is normally the case, the words of Jesus express it best:

> *The kings of the Gentiles lord it over them; and those who exercise authority over them call themselves Benefactors. But you are not to be like that. Instead, the greatest among you should be like the youngest, and the one who rules like the one who serves. For who is greater, the one who is at the table or the one who serves? Is it not the one who is at the table? But I am among you as one who serves.* (Luke 22:25-27)

Stand for People

As a result of the sinful behavior of the Israelites, God actually declares to Moses that He would destroy them and make a great nation out of Moses. Well, let's consider that just a moment. Here is Moses' chance. These people have done nothing but complain and battle against him from the beginning. They have been a pain to work with and consistently ungrateful. They seem to instantly forget God's miracles and

Moses' sacrifices. Maybe Moses should take God up on this offer? On the surface, it certainly seems to be a better deal than constantly putting up with the grumbling and complaining of these people who God rightly calls *"stiff-necked!"* But that isn't Moses' reaction. "Moses's first reaction is to defend them against divine rage" (Grumet 2014, 46). Moses, by his nature, comes to the defense of his people.

Let's be honest here. People can be a pain. They can be grumbling, complaining, ungrateful, and petty. As one frustrated pastor puts it, "Ministry would be perfect if it weren't for the people!" Actually that isn't a true statement. In reality, ministry cannot exist without the people. In fact, leadership cannot exist without people. As pastors, we are not in the theology business or the social reconstruction business. We are in the people business. God loves people. While He can become angry and frustrated with humankind, His love for us knows no bounds. Therefore, as the physical manifestation of the presence of the Holy Spirit to this world, we must show the same love and concern for people, even when they are difficult and borderline impossible. When my wife and I first entered ministry, we took a part-time role as a youth pastor at a very small church. They youth group in this church was made up almost entirely of teens brought in by the church van each week. These kids did not have family in the church and were, in fact, almost entirely from broken and dysfunctional homes. They were not easy to work with. There were times when we would be forced to physically restrain one student in order to protect the safety of another. One day, while visiting Tina's mom and dad, I lamented to her father about the difficult situation. "We just can't seem to get through to these kids. They just don't respond to the love we are trying so hard to show them." To this, Tina's father replied, "Mike, those kids have heard people say they love them their entire lives only to have those same people leave them a few months later. There has been almost no stability. Where there is stability, there is often abuse. Perhaps what they are looking for is longevity. Perhaps they are thinking: 'You say you love me? Fine. Let me mistreat you and see if you stay. Then I will believe you love me.'" That turned the light on in my mind. These kids, like the Israelites, had never seen kind and loving leadership. They didn't know what it looked like and couldn't recognize it when it happened. They needed to test our sincerity first before they would expose their hearts. The people of Israel needed to see Moses stand up for them, just like the people in your church need to see you stand up for them. When they see how much you love them, they will allow you the right to lead them. Until then, you are just another insincere overlord using them to accomplish your own hopes and dreams. So, stand by them and love them, even when they are truly *"a stiff-necked people."*

BE GOD'S MAN

> *The LORD would speak to Moses face to face, as one speaks to a friend.*
>
> *—Exodus 33:11*

The upward development pattern occurs throughout a leader's life. It is a spiral of growth in being and doing. In each *being* cycle there is an increased depth of experience and knowing God; and in each *doing* cycle there is increased depth of effective service for God. The final result of the upward development pattern is a fusion of being and doing.

—Dr. J. Robert Clinton, *The Making of a Leader*

Spiritual leadership is different from secular leadership. Today, as we look across the spectrum of leaders that our society celebrates, we find people who are really only concerned with winning. There is little sense of right and wrong, only a vague notion of good and bad. However, there is an overwhelming emphasis on winning. The athlete can lack integrity and kindness, as long as he scores the points needed to win. The politician can lack truthfulness and transparency, as long as he lies better than the opponent and wins. The businessman can lack fairness and compassion, as long as he meets or exceeds the bottom line. Today, leadership seems to be all about winning, but that isn't how it should work in the realm of spiritual leadership. As a Christian leader, our primary goal is never winning. It is always becoming. Now, don't get me wrong. There is nothing unspiritual about success and winning. Those things are fine, and God wants to bring His people to victory. It's when we allow winning to overcome our desire to become more like God and closer to Him that we fail. In fact, in spiritual leadership, you can win the game, make the money, and hold the office all while losing at the primary goal of becoming more like our model of proper living, Christ. Our goal, in the spiritual world, is less about winning and more about becoming.

Now, becoming more like Christ is a lifelong process. It is not something that we are going to achieve at a weekend retreat or by responding to an altar call after a great and moving sermon. No, it is all about years of learning to press out of our existence those things that are not of God and draw into our existence those things that are of God. In writing about leadership development, Dr. J. Robert Clinton puts it this way: "Leadership is a lifetime of God's lessons. Yours will be unique. God will take you through several 'leadership stages' on your way to a lifetime of service" (Clinton 1988, 27). The daily goal of each spiritual leader then should be to minimize the effect in our lives of things that make us less like God and maximize the things in our lives that make us more like God. Let's take a look at just a few areas in which we must continually work.

Completely Remove Idols

"They [Israelites] have been quick to turn away from what I commanded them and have made themselves an idol cast in the shape of a calf." (Exodus 32:8)

Idolatry and worship of anything but God is something that He just cannot abide. Throughout Scripture, it is clear that God will not allow His people to worship anyone or anything but Him. The reason is really far simpler than most people make it out to be. It is only God who desires to make you better, and it is only the God of the Bible who can build you into all that He made you to be. All other gods, all other worship, all other efforts are weak and pale in comparison with what God wants to do in our lives. When the Israelites build a golden calf and begin to worship it saying, *"These are your gods, Israel, who brought you up out of Egypt"* (Exodus 32:4), they insult the very presence of the Lord God of Heaven who actually did bring them up out of Egypt. Now they intend to depend on this dead piece of metal to lead them. *"Come, make us gods who will go before us"* (Exodus 32:1). Somehow these Israelites are not simply expecting this golden calf to represent the presence of God among them; they are looking for this metal statue to impart the direction of God to them. They are asking to be lied to, since that is the only way nonliving things can speak to living things. Should Moses not return and Aaron need to lead the people from this point forward, Aaron will simply declare his words to have come from the calf. In this way, Aaron will be able to force the people to do what he wants by lying to them about whose voice they are hearing. Now, I don't think Aaron was planning to take the ruse that far. I think he was just trying to buy enough time for Moses to return. Others have done exactly this, and still do.

Idolatry works that way. Someone convinces us to set something up in our life that is more important to us than God. We then set that thing in the middle of our existence, the place God should occupy. We listen to the voice of the one who convinced us all the while believing it is the voice of the idol we set up. Nonliving things don't talk to living things. Moses knows this. He realizes that the calf has no real power, no real authority, and no real voice. The people have chosen to attribute a voice to this nonliving thing. "From the top of the mountain, as he defends his people, Moses can view the calf as being sheer farce, telling God that it lacks all power and is not real. But standing below, Moses senses the power and vitality that Israel imputes to the calf, and he can't help but become infuriated" (Cohen 2007, 117). Once Moses realizes that the Israelites have attributed a voice to this nonliving statue, Moses must take devastatingly swift and decisive action to remedy the situation.

In our lives as leaders, we can sometimes be duped into attributing power to nonliving things. Things like money, authority, fame, and power call to us in what seems to be a living voice. In reality, it is nothing more than the voice of Satan, the deceiver. His goal is *"to steal and kill and destroy"* (John 10:10). His influence must be negated in devastatingly swift and decisive ways. Our ability to lead in a godly manner will be negated by the presence of an idol in our lives. Whatever the reason that the idol has been allowed in, it must be driven out and destroyed. I often ask our church members to view the nation of Israel as an individual and not as a nation when trying to learn from the Old Testament accounts. That practice applied here gives insight to how swiftly and determinedly we should encounter any idol once we look and realize that we have given it undue authority in our lives. *"Then he [Moses] said to them, 'This is what the LORD, the God of Israel, says: "Each man strap a sword to his side. Go back and forth through the camp from one end to the other, each killing his brother and friend and neighbor"'"* (Exodus 32:27). This command is brutal and some have been unable to even receive it as having been from the mouth of God. "One *midrash* even suggests that Moses's zealotry at the Golden Calf was a sin even worse than the Golden Calf itself" (Grumet 2014, 47). For our purposes, imagine this as an internal spiritual battle. One must, with resolve, enter into the realms of the heart and utterly destroy those things that are attempting to take the place of God and replace the voice of God in your life. There is no place for simply managing these destructive gods. They must be killed, destroyed, and sent out, no matter how dear they have become to us. This way we find our dependence and direction fully focused and fully devoted to the God who wishes to set us free. We get there by revolution. A revolution that slays the internal spiritual slaveholder. A revolution that takes back the place where only God should sit and re-establishes the voice (in the spiritual leader's life) that should be the only voice in our lives.

Stay Close to the Holy Spirit

"Then Moses said to him [God], 'If your Presence does not go with us, do not send us up from here. How will anyone know that you are pleased with me and with your people unless you go with us? What else will distinguish me and your people from all the other people on the face of the earth?'" (Exodus 33:15-16)

I am no good by myself. I love having my wife with me at all times. When she is not around, I find it difficult to sleep and life just isn't right. I am just no good by myself. I wonder sometimes if this isn't just a small image of what Moses was feeling when God told him to *"Leave this place, you and the people you brought up out of Egypt ... But I will not go with you, because you are a stiff-necked people and I might destroy you on the way"* (Exodus 33:1-3). God was sending Moses and the Israelites away from His presence because of their sin. Moses, having had nothing to do with the sinful behavior, is now faced with leading the nation alone without the guiding and empowering presence of God. This is not, in his mind, a workable solution. There is no way that Moses could possibly lead these people without God. He has struggled enough with God around. What will he ever accomplish on his own? So Moses implores God to allow him and the people to remain near to His presence.

As spiritual leaders, we should desire the presence of God with identical intensity. The situations are the same. We are faced with a leadership task that is impossible for us to accomplish on our own. The prospect of attempting to lead at this level without the presence of God should be terrifying, especially when the people we lead are even more prone to angering God. It isn't like God is looking for a way to leave His people. He actually worked on their behalf to get to them and deliver them from their bondage. However, their hearts are not fully committed to Him. That is where the failure comes in. Moses, through personal time with God, has developed a love for God that is now strong and growing. The people either from lack of time or lack of interest have not yet developed this love relationship with God. That makes meaningful obedience virtually impossible.

> If you have an obedience problem, you have a love problem. Focus your attention on God's love. Could you stand before God and describe your relationship to Him by saying, "I love You with all my heart and all my soul and all my mind and all my strength"? Jesus said He would take those who respond to His love into an ever-deepening experience of love and fellowship with Him. (Blackaby et al. 2008, 81)

Time with God and time pursuing God can solve this dilemma. As leaders, we must realize that our people pursue God, in most cases, to a lesser degree than we do. Let's say on a scale of 1 to 10 with ten being fully surrendered to God and fully filled with the Holy Spirit, you desire for the people you lead to reach at least a level 6. This will mean that you must be beyond that. Some of them will exceed you, but most will not. If you desire to have a church filled with level 6 followers of Christ, then you must consistently exhibit levels of personal relationship with God that reach beyond a level 8 and attain a 10. I don't mean to coldly rate the level of our commitment to Christ. Such rating scales are not really possible. However, I need to make the point that our desire for the presence of God should be at the highest possible intensity. Honestly, the prospect of trying to lead without Him is terrifying.

Seek God's Presence

"Then Moses said, 'Now show me your glory.'" (Exodus 33:18)

Our primary goal in our spiritual leadership should be an ever deeper and more intimate experience of the presence and power of God. Years ago, I was talking to a mentor of mine and he told me how he had been praying for me. At the time, his prayers actually frightened me. "Mike, I am praying that you will experience the power of God with such intensity in your ministry that you could not possibly control or contain what He is accomplishing around and through you." Honestly, my first thought was that I wanted him to stop praying for me! Then he explained further. "If you ever once experience God's presence and power in that way, you will never be satisfied with anything less." He was right. I have seen moments where the power and presence of the Holy Spirit in and around my life and ministry have been nothing short of frightening. I have approached meetings concerning future ministry opportunities that no one knew about, only to receive a text on the way to the meeting telling me that the Holy Spirit was opening a door to the opportunity and I should walk through the door without fear. No one knew about the meeting!! But the Holy Spirit did. I have been praying for a family member only to have someone walk up and say: "Pastor, your family member has been on my mind and the Holy Spirit wants me to tell you it's going to be OK." I have even had moments when I was wrestling with intense personal and professional choices that were highly risky and dangerous only to have someone tell me: "I know you are worried right now, but God wants me to tell you that it's OK and you should go forward without fear." No one knew about any of these things, yet someone spoke into them at the exact moment. The Holy Spirit moved. These moments do not somehow indicate that I am important or powerful. They actually indicate the opposite. I don't know what to do, but the Holy Spirit does. Quite often, the Spirit will not tell me what to do next lest I should begin to believe that I have it all figured out. Instead, He lets me squirm in my indecision and insecurities just long enough to remember my need for Him. Then He sends his message from someone else to let me know that He is always present. Having now experienced that kind of power in spiritual leadership, I would rather quit ministry than ever attempt to lead His people without His presence.

In his book, *Movements That Changed The World*, Steve Addison points out the following: "Profound encounters with God are important catalysts in the formation of movements for the renewal and expansion of the Christian faith" (Addison 2011, 38). If we desire a true movement of the Holy Spirit that can actually change the hearts, minds, and practices of our culture and move our people toward an ever deepening walk with the Holy Spirit, it is going to require a lifetime of "profound encounters with God." These encounters are the lifeblood of the spiritual leader's capacity to lead. They give encouragement and authority to the work of the spiritual leader and drive us forward no matter how hot and dry the desert of the day may be. Once having sat on the mountaintop with God, we desire more. *"Show me your glory"* becomes the life call of the leader who has diligently sat on the mountain listening to the heart of the Master. Finally, the day comes. The Holy Spirit moves into the room we occupy with such force and presence that we desire, even need, a *"cleft in the rock"* (Exodus 33:22) where we can press ever further into the stone underneath the pressing presence of the God of Heaven. In those moments, we realize that we desire that which we could never actually handle. *"Then I will remove my hand and you will see my back; but my face must not be seen"* (Exodus 33:23). A quick passing glance at the back of God is the closest any human has ever come to actually seeing God this side of eternity. Yet, that was all humanity could handle of an encounter with the infinite, eternal power and presence of the Creator God of Heaven. But that was enough. Moses realized that it was all he could take, and even that set a fire in his heart and set the very countenance of his face ablaze. Moses encountered the very presence of God, and everyone could tell! Now that is a powerful place from which to lead!

MINISTRY OF PRESENCE

> *When Moses came down from Mount Sinai with the two tablets of the covenant law in his hands, he was not aware that his face was radiant because he had spoken with the LORD. When Aaron and all the Israelites saw Moses, his face was radiant, and they were afraid to come near him. But Moses called to them; so Aaron and all the leaders of the community came back to him, and he spoke to them. Afterward all the Israelites came near him, and he gave them all the commands the LORD had given him on Mount Sinai. When Moses finished speaking to them, he put a veil over his face.*
>
> *—Exodus 34:29-33*

The hiding of God's face is part of what, in the human experience, distinguishes God from people. It unambiguously establishes God as Other, with whom there can be no face-to-face dialogue or meeting of equals. God is not the equal of anyone or anything. Similarly, the hiding of Moses's face soon afterwards sends a parallel message — Moses is not an equal of anyone, and in his uniqueness, he is removed from the ordinariness of his people. The qualitative distance between God and Moses is mirrored in the distance between Moses and the people generated by the masking of Moses. In an ironic twist of self-fulfilling prophecy, through the incident of the Golden Calf, Moses becomes the God-like figure for whom the people initially sought a replacement when they thought that they had lost him.

—Zvi Grumet, *Moses and the Path to Leadership*

One of the great privileges of my life is that God allowed me to be part of the family in which I was born. I have spoken of these things on so many occasions, but it is core to who I am and why I am able to lead. Both of my grandfathers were Wesleyan pastors, one in North Carolina and one in South Carolina. My Grandfather Freeman was a Wesleyan pastor from North Carolina. I received Christ as my Savior for the first time in the church he pastored after a sermon he preached. What I most remember about him was when he would pray. Grandpa Freeman was one of those rare people that would walk in to a room and literally change the atmosphere. He was not gregarious or ever the center of attention, but he was a man who spent great amounts of time with God. One Sunday, I had returned to our home church for Sunday services. As the worship moved forward, it became obvious that the Holy Spirit was going to do something special in that service. As the presence of the Holy Spirit became stronger in the room, Grandpa stood up from his seat in the audience. He had been retired from active ministry for years and had just recently been through surgery. He was weak and feeble due to his advanced age and health concerns. But still, he stood up. As he began to talk, the church fell amazingly and deafeningly silent. Every person in the room realized that God was about to speak to us through him. He began to walk away from his seat and into the aisle as his voice grew in intensity and power. This was not at all like him. He just wasn't a person who took much spotlight. Then as his voice grew ever stronger and the Spirit obviously began to move even more powerfully through him, he began to kick up his heels and give further praise to his God. I don't remember anything he said that day. I do remember the power of the Holy Spirit freely flowing through Grandpa. As he began to wrap up, he stopped right in front of the entire church and took hold of me praising God for me and the rest of the family. He embraced me as we both cried and praised the God of Heaven.

I will never forget that moment.

Decades later, I was invited to a meeting for which I had always dreamed of receiving an invitation. Within our denominational tribe, the Wesleyans, we used to hold an annual gathering of the lead pastors of our largest churches. I was invited for the first time, so Tina and I packed up and traveled to the meeting. On the opening night of the meeting, all the pastors gathered in a room. The goal of this first meeting was to get to know each other, especially the new guys. I was a new guy. I listened as each of these men (all heroes to me) spoke of their ministry and what God was doing in and through them. I sat there a little star-struck, a little intimidated, and with a ton of questions of how I got here. Then suddenly, it was my turn. I began to explain who I was and what God had been doing in and through us at New Life, and as I spoke, I did the very last thing anyone in that position wants to do. As I sat there, in a meeting I had longed to be a part of my entire career, surrounded by many of my heroes in ministry and the faith, I melted into tears. To this day, I'm not entirely sure what the tears were all about. Looking back, I can say this. In that room, I learned that these leaders are as impressive as anyone may have expected. They are all brilliant, talented leaders with a powerful presence and sincere hearts. But they were just leaders, like me. I may have been intimidated. I may have just been overwhelmed. I may have been suffering from jet lag. (Turned out this first meeting was held in Hawaii! God is good!) Whatever the real reason for melting into tears, I can tell you what I realized that day and have realized many more times in many more rooms with many more heroes. When I'm old, I don't want to be any of them.

I want to be Grandpa Freeman.

I have been part of that group for more than a decade, and I can tell you that they all feel the same way. They don't long to be my Grandpa Freeman, but every one of them has a Grandpa Freeman. They are all impressive, and just to be allowed in the same room with them is an honor that I could never deserve. However, I want to glow from the presence of the Holy Spirit in my own life and heart. I want to silence a room, not because I am Pastor Mike or a respected leader. I want to silence a room because the entire room looks up and sees right past me and realizes that the Holy Spirit is about to speak. They realize that He will speak through me, but they don't see me. They see Him. They know that they will hear my voice, but they will hear His words. They trust that after all that time in the presence of God, humility and surrender will hide pride and release truth. A leader like that will glow, without even realizing that the awesome power of God is flowing through him. That leader will just glow with the presence of the Holy Spirit. Moses didn't even realize that *"his face was radiant."* Grandpa didn't even realize that he silenced an entire room. Both of them just knew they had been with God and had something to say. The glow makes people uncomfortable, but it also leaves them silent. It leaves them somehow knowing that they will now hear from God, and the glow they see on this face is the residue of the Spirit's presence. That kind of residual glow only comes after long, uninterrupted periods of time in the presence of the Almighty. That kind of residual glow generates respect, direction, wisdom, and authority. I have much left to accomplish and many leadership experiences yet to go through. I realize the following is true: "Spiritual leaders work within a paradox, for God calls them to do something that, in fact, only God can do. Ultimately, spiritual leaders cannot produce spiritual change in people; only the Holy Spirit can accomplish this. Yet the Spirit often uses people to bring about spiritual growth in others" (Blackaby 2001, 21). What we are called to do is not possible for us to accomplish. Then again, this is nothing new with God. When He assigns the impossible task,

He provides the undeniable glow, if we do the work of finding unhindered surrender in His unending presence. During that time in His presence, He fills and empowers until, even without realizing it, the spiritual leader becomes simply radiant with the Spirit's presence. I want to do so much. When it is all said and done, I don't want to be remembered as anything but a man through whom God could shine radiantly. The glow is the goal.

LEADERSHIP IS BY LEADER, NOT COMMITTEE

> *Now Moses was a very humble man, more humble than anyone else on the face of the earth.*
>
> —*Numbers 12:3*

Decision making is a fundamental responsibility of leaders. People who are unwilling or unable to make decisions are unlikely leadership candidates. Leaders may consult counselors; they may seek consensus from their people; they may gather further information; but ultimately they must make choices. Leaders who refuse to do so are abdicating their leadership role. People need the assurance that their leader is capable of making wise, timely decisions.

—Henry and Richard Blackaby, *Spiritual Leadership*

Throughout Moses' life, he faces leadership challenges. Like any leader, the challenges are different at each stage of leadership development and must be navigated in its own unique way. As Moses navigated these challenges, he did so with a humility that constantly leaned on the wisdom, power, and direction of the Holy Spirit. Leaders simply must function with a humble attitude. While this may seem like a disconnect from reality, the truth is that leadership carries great costs that the leader must be willing to pay. If the leader insists on a seat of power and comfort, the ability to actually lead will be diminished by the arrogance of believing that power and comfort are deserved. Instead, in humility, leaders must be willing to pay the price of leadership. "Many people today want to climb up the corporate ladder because they believe that freedom, power, and wealth are the prizes waiting at the top. The life of a leader can look glamorous to people on the outside. But the reality is that leadership requires sacrifice" (Maxwell 2007, 222). The price of leadership would perhaps be easier to pay if it were charged in monetary measures, or even in actual blood. However, that isn't how it tends to happen. Leaders are challenged most often in the very areas God has called them to function. In fact, leaders are often challenged in the very areas where they have already displayed strength and ability. By the time we reach chapters 12-20 of Numbers, Moses has firmly established himself as the leader of the nation of Israel. God has performed many miracles through Moses and has clearly shown that Moses is His chosen leader. Yet, even now, Moses faces challenges to his authority and use of power. Moses, in the face of these four instances of rebellion against his authority, must strike the delicate balance between power and grace. Striking this balance is far more art than science. There are times when the leader must act in absolute authority in order to ensure the safe and successful completion of the mission at hand. There are other times when grace must be used in great doses in order to ensure that the people who need to remain on point are able to remain on point. At first glance, it may seem that grace and power cannot simultaneously coexist in a decision making process. But they can. "Here's the paradox: flourishing comes from being both strong and weak. Flourishing requires us to embrace both authority and vulnerability, both capacity and frailty—even, at least in this broken world, both life and death" (Crouch 2016, 11). As Moses faces significant challenges to his leadership and even questioning of his divine call and authority, he must work to artfully strike the proper balance between power and grace.

Practice Grace

"Miriam and Aaron began to talk against Moses because of his Cushite wife, for he had married a Cushite. 'Has the LORD spoken only through Moses?' they asked. 'Hasn't he also spoken through us?' And the LORD heard this." (Numbers 12:1-2)

This challenging period in Moses' life begins with what must have been one of the most painful challenges that Moses will face in his life as a leader.

Painful Shots from Close Range

Miriam and Aaron, Moses's sister and brother, are calling into question his authority as the leader of Israel. They are doing so using two deeply hurtful accusations. As a pastoral leader, you should always remember that the most painful opposition you will ever face comes from the people who are closest to you. It's actually devastating. When people who live on the periphery of your life make accusations, it is a nuisance. When people in your inner circle make accusations, it is earth shattering. The pain comes because those closest to you know exactly where to strike when they choose to do so. Miriam and Aaron question Moses' spiritual authority by asking if he is the only one who God can speak through and use. They doubt his moral authority by questioning his marriage to a non-Jewish wife. Neither of these are valid arguments. God has already been speaking through both Moses and Aaron, and Moses was married to Zipporah long before even the burning bush event. The accusations have staying power because they drive to the natural tendency of humankind to find fault with those in front. The fact that this comes from family makes it all the more painful. That pain cannot be allowed to consume you or cause you to react in the wrong manner. You must remember two very difficult truths in these moments.

You cannot stop following God's call just because those closest to you lose faith in you.

You cannot simply crush those who are closest to you without deep regret later on.

Quiet Pain Standing in Hopeful Faith

In order for both of these to remain true in your life and leadership, you must choose your reaction carefully. You must find the artful balance between grace and justice. Honestly, I suppose there are few moments more difficult to navigate than this balance. In this difficult moment, Moses, a man who often reacts in passionate anger or decisive justice, shows tremendous restraint.

> As hurtful as Miriam's remarks are to Moses, he restrains himself. Occasionally, as we have seen, he does respond angrily when Israel challenges him. But Aaron and Miriam are his brother and sister, whom he loves, and he is sensitive to the people's perception of them. God also responds rather leniently to Miriam and Aaron's remarks, as seen in the Divine's first words of chastisement: "Hear, I pray you (na), my words" (12:6). The simple word na (please) ostensibly bears the meaning of a request. (Cohen 2007, 126)

Restraint in moments like this can give room for God to do what we could not. Moses does not react to Miriam and Aaron's claims, but the Bible makes it clear that *"the LORD heard this."*

At this point, God gets personally involved. He calls a meeting of the three of them and clearly communicates that Moses is the leader God has appointed. This leadership position does not diminish the tremendous level of authority and blessing that God has bestowed on Miriam and Aaron, but it does clearly establish the lines of leadership that God insists are followed. Notice as you look through his account that Moses says nothing. At no point has Moses argued with Miriam and Aaron or even defended himself. Moses simply trusts that God is going to work this out. I think this level of confidence that God will work out our most hurtful moments in leadership is an extremely difficult level of maturity to learn and practice. Yet, Moses quietly waits. He does not argue, imprison, fight against, or even speak about Miriam and Aaron and their rebellion. He just waits for God to deal with it. And God does. After making it abundantly clear that Moses is the leader and clearly displaying the intimacy with which God speaks to Moses, God asks what must have been a terrifying question to Miriam and Aaron: *"Why then were you not afraid to speak against my servant Moses?"* (Numbers 12:8). While this verse should never be abused in an effort to shut out debate or accountability, it must be recognized for the truth it contains. When God is working through a given leader, if you choose to oppose that leader, you have chosen to oppose God. If I may be very direct here, opposing God never ends well. *"The anger of the LORD burned against them, and he left them. When the cloud lifted from above the tent, Miriam's skin was leprous—it became as white as snow"* (Numbers 12:9-10).

Forgiveness and Healing

When Aaron sees the leprosy that has overtaken Miriam, he is horrified. They both suddenly realize their mistake and the extreme cost of that mistake. They realize that they have not been speaking against Moses alone, but also against God. Now, there is a price to pay. Moses does no gloating in this obvious vindication of his leadership. He is as horrified as Aaron at the leprosy that has overtaken his sister. Rather than let go of a barrage of "I told you so," Moses instantly begins to plead with God for Miriam's healing. *"So Moses cried out to the LORD, 'Please, God, heal her!'"* (Numbers 12:13). However, the healing will come at a price. God demands that Miriam be kept outside the camp for seven days until she is healed of the leprosy. During those seven days, the entire nation of Israel waits for Miriam. The sin of Miriam and Aaron has been laid bare before the entire nation, but not by Moses, by God. Once healing has come, Moses has the opportunity to receive her back into the nation, healed, forgiven, and whole. Scripture doesn't give us a description of the day that Miriam re-enters the camp, but I can imagine that Moses was the first to greet her. Sincere grace does that. It forgives, it implores for healing, and once that healing has come, it restores.

Practice Decisiveness

"But the men who had gone up with him [Caleb] said, 'We can't attack these people; they are stronger than we are.' And they spread among the Israelites a bad report about the land they had explored…. That night all the members of the community raised their voices and wept aloud. All the Israelites grumbled against Moses and Aaron, and the whole assembly said to them, 'If only we had died in Egypt!'" (Numbers 13:31-32, 14:1-2)

Now, Moses faces a very different challenge to his authority. Having been told by the Lord to send spies into the Promised Land, Moses chose a representative from each of the tribes of Israel to see what was facing the nation as they entered the land. Upon their return, they verify that this land *"does flow with milk and honey!"* (Numbers 13:27). They even bring samples of the fruit of the land back with them for the nation to see. However, the majority of the spies, 10 out of the 12, are more afraid of the current inhabitants than they are impressed by the beauty and productivity of the land. These ten strike great fear into the hearts of the people, and oddly enough, Moses seems to have no response. It seems that he and Aaron simply sit by and listen as the entire plan to enter their Promised Land falls apart. The people become completely rebellious and in fear refuse to move forward. They choose to fear the inhabitants of the land more than they trust their God and Moses. Moses offers nothing to encourage them. In his book, *Moses and the Path to Leadership*, Grumet paints an effective picture of what Moses' failure to lead decisively must have looked like:

> Moses's weakness as a leader of people haunts him with every twist of this story. When the spies first deliver their report, it is Calev, not Moses, who understands the implications of their presentation. Calev quiets the people so that they can listen to Moses's anticipated words: "Calev silenced the people around Moses and said, 'We will surely go up and take hold of [the land], for we will sure prevail over [the inhabitants]'" (Numbers 13:30). Yet the pregnant silence Calev creates is broken not by Moses, but by the ten reporting spies as they rile up the crowds…. From Moses we hear absolutely nothing." (Grumet 2014, 112)

This lack of decisiveness on Moses' part allows the sense of despair caused by the report of the 10 negative spies to sink deep into the hearts of the Israelites. They lose hope, and then Moses seems to lose nerve. After an entire night of wailing and mourning, Moses goes out only to encounter a people who are ready to kill him and Aaron and appoint a leader to take them back to Egypt. *"Then Moses and Aaron fell facedown in front of the whole Israelite assembly gathered there"* (Numbers 14:5). Again, Moses is silent. Face to the ground, he and Aaron just seem defeated. Perhaps they were exhausted, or perhaps they, too, were convinced that the Israelites were no match for the current inhabitants of the Promised Land. Whatever the reason, the leaders were frozen and unable to lead. Joshua and Caleb do their best to rally the people and lead in Moses and Aaron's absence, but this falls short. While Moses, miraculously, remains the leader of the Israelites, this has obviously not been a good moment in his leadership journey. "In his handling of the crowds, Moses clearly and repeatedly needs outside help, and even then he is not successful until his Protector and Benefactor steps in" (Grumet 2014, 113).

When God-appointed leaders fail to lead in crisis moments, a devastating level of confusion and fear sets in. Had Moses stepped up and spoken with Caleb and Joshua, then perhaps the people could have been convinced and a generation could have been saved. But Moses did not step up. Only when God intervened did the people stop planning for a return to their bondage. The lesson here for the leader is clear.

When God has given you a task, stand your ground and lead. The people God has charged you with leading need you. They will lose heart without you. If you fail to show them the way to God's Promised Land, they will crawl back to their captors and willingly return to slavery. We simply must lead. There is no doubt that what God has called us to is terrifying and beyond our capacity. There is no doubt that the land God has called us to occupy is infested with giants and warriors. There is no doubt that without the miraculous intervention of God, we will fail. But God will not fail. He will intervene when we are following His call. With God on our side, there are no giants or warriors that stand a chance! So, leader, if God has called you, get off your face and break the silence of fear with the voice of faith God has already placed within you. If you don't, you could lose a generation of progress.

Practice Strength

"They came as a group to oppose Moses and Aaron and said to them, 'You have gone too far! The whole community is holy, every one of them, and the LORD is with them. Why then do you set yourselves above the LORD's assembly?'" (Numbers 16:3)

Once again, Moses' leadership is questioned. A rebellion is rising up among the people primarily led by Korah, Dathan, and Abiram. These men, and those who are following them, are making similar claims to the ones made by Miriam and Aaron; they are questioning Moses' spiritual authority to lead the people of Israel. This instance is different in a few ways. Miriam and Aaron seem to have wanted a greater share of the authority to lead the nation, but they did not seem to be looking for Moses to be removed from leadership. These men wish to overthrow Moses' authority and lead the nation themselves. To further complicate things, this event occurs after the failure of the nation to enter the Promised Land. There is no doubt that strong leaders within the nation observed Moses and Aaron as they lacked the fortitude to lead the nation forward into the Promised Land. While these angry leaders may have agreed that the nation should not go forward, the weakness of leadership displayed by Moses and Aaron caused a rebellious nature to rise up in Korah, Dathan, and Abiram. As they began to envision different ways in which the nation could be led, they began to attract more and more of the people who were somehow connected to or loyal to them as supporters. Until finally, there is a sufficient uprising to demand an audience with Moses. This kind of uprising is, unfortunately, not uncommon in churches. After viewing a moment where the leader failed to show proper leadership, strength, or direction, another leader (or two) rises up convinced that they can do the job better. As for the issue of God's calling, they simply throw out that classic line, *"The whole community is holy, every one of them, and the LORD is with them. Why then do you set yourselves above the LORD's assembly?"* In other words, they want to call for a vote. If they can get a vote of no confidence in Moses and Aaron, then they can take over. Folks like these gain strength by engaging their inner circles and then slowly working their way outward to infect others.

> Familial ties lead to strong homogeneous bonds that may form natural groups within the church. These groups may have tendencies to think, act, and respond in similar manner. Seniority, prestige, position, or wealth among members or leadership may provide the credential for those individuals to be internal leaders with significant influence. (Petersen et al. 2010, 226)

Once these various groupings of power players have cemented together, there is going to be a fight.

In moments like these, most leaders will tend to default to a similar form of crisis management like the one we observed with Miriam and Aaron. However, that would be a mistake. Remember that Miriam and Aaron were not looking to overthrow Moses. They were not looking to change the fundamental God-appointed direction of the nation of Israel. They simply wanted more credit for what was going on or more say in what would happen next. Korah and his people are not trying to play a larger role in what God is already doing; they want to alter the course of action entirely. They are basically saying, "We do not believe that the present course of action is God's will." They are convinced that God is no longer speaking to Moses. The problem is that they don't really have a plan either. These people seem to want to simply have a democratic vote to see which way the nation should go. Democracy is a wonderful thing. It has served as the basis of our freedom in this wonderful nation for centuries. However, can you imagine what would happen if Americans were a nomadic group of former slaves wandering around in the desert? Every time it got too hot, we would elect a new leader. If the water ran low, elect a new leader. If the quail sent by God got too skinny, elect a new leader. If the dust blew the wrong way, elect a new leader. Had the Israelites taken this approach, they may still be wandering around that desert today! No, leadership comes from leaders. Godly leadership comes from God-appointed leaders. In moments of crisis, leadership by a leader is imperative. Committees no longer are effective in crisis moments. Let's be honest. The entire journey from Egypt to the Promised Land, all forty years of it, was lived out in crisis. Always needing water, food, shelter, and protection, the people lived in constant crisis. They did not need a committee that would lead by consensus; they needed a leader that would lead by the guidance and power of God.

Therefore, given the grace nature of this threat not only to Moses' leadership but also to the ultimate direction of the nation, Moses was forced to face this one directly, swiftly, and harshly. Moses, knowing what was required to win back the hearts of his people, stands his ground firmly and publicly against these rebellious leaders. He then trusts God to show up and take care of the situation. With Korah and his followers, Moses watches as God destroys them with fire for presenting an unworthy sacrifice before the Lord. As for Dathan and Abiram, Moses asks God to do something that has never been seen before. As Moses moves the nation away from the tents of Dathan and Abiram, *"the ground under them split apart and the earth opened its mouth and swallowed them"* (Numbers 16:31-32). Moses, knowing that he was called of God and certain that God was not finished with him in this place of leadership, stands his ground firmly and sees God validate his leadership in the most dramatic of ways. This Moses, who seemed to have no words a few chapters ago, now finds his courage and stands his ground. "The very fact that Moses came up with this idea and stood firm in the face of his antagonists again points to a radical change in his self-perception as a leader" (Grumet 2014, 121-122). Perhaps we need such a change in our perception of God's calling for us? Perhaps as we balance grace and decisiveness in leadership, we can learn to lead with strength in right and righteous ways.

Practice Patience

"Now there was no water for the community, and the people gathered in opposition to Moses and Aaron. They quarreled with Moses and said, 'If only we had died when our brothers fell dead before the LORD! Why did you bring the LORD's community into this wilderness, that we and our livestock should die here?'... The LORD said to Moses, 'Take the staff, and you and your brother Aaron gather the assembly together. Speak to that rock before their eyes and it will pour out its water.... So Moses took the staff from the LORD's presence, just as he commanded him. He and Aaron gathered the assembly together in front of the rock and Moses said to them, 'Listen, you rebels, must we bring you water out of this rock?' Then Moses raised his arm and struck the rock twice with his staff. Water gushed out, and the community and their livestock drank." (Numbers 20:2-4, 7-11)

Unfortunately, we once again find an illustration from the life of Moses teaching us how not to handle a situation. It should be encouraging to us to realize that one of the greatest leaders in all of human history made so many mistakes. We do not have to be perfect to lead, just surrendered. Moses did not do everything right, and when he got it wrong, it cost him dearly.

As we enter the story here in Numbers 20, we must realize that a great deal of time has passed. We have jumped perhaps 20-30 or more years between chapter 19 and chapter 20 of Numbers. "One significant gap for which the *midrash* has little to say covers a thirty-eight year period of the Israelites in the wilderness" (Grumet 2014, 129). Here, in the first verse of chapter 20, we find that Miriam, Moses and Aaron's sister, has died. It is in the throes of mourning the loss of their sister that Moses and Aaron now face a familiar sound, the grumbling of Israel. Whether it is because of his grief at the loss of his sister, or because it has been so long since such rancorous complaints have been heard, Moses seems surprisingly incapable to properly handle the situation.

> By now we would expect Moses to be able to distinguish between justified complaints and unwarranted challenges. Moses should also be aware that this is a different people, that this is a completely new generation. It seems, however, that Moses does not see them as different. He is impatient with them, calling them the rebellious ones — even though this is

the first recorded complaint in thirty-eight years. And when God instructs him to *speak* to the rock, Moses resorts to hitting the rock as he did in the first days after the exodus. For Moses himself, this is a return to his old ways of viewing the people and reacting to them. (Grumet 2014, 96)

The truth is that as leaders we are all given a big stick. It is the symbol of our power and can be used as a defensive weapon, an offensive weapon, or as a simple deterrent. The wisdom comes in knowing how to use that weapon. Now, some within the church refuse to admit that such power is at work in the hands of a pastor or lay leader. They are mistaken.

Given the fact that the church is a place of intense human interaction, it should be no surprise that power comes into play there often. It is implicit in our relationships as brothers and sisters in Christ. Yet we often ignore the reality of power in the church. While a healthy distrust of power may be a good thing, the denial of its existence can only lead to the abuse of power. (Schmidt 2006, 149-150)

The seat of our power as leaders must be handled properly or we can quickly become guilty of abusing that power. As pastors, once we have abused the power God has given us, we often will lose that power. If once you strike out in anger, your moral authority is gone. Then the power you hold is significantly diminished. I have personally fallen victim to this. There have been times in my career that I have failed to control my anger and released it in simple torrents of frustration. I could give you reasons why these events took place, and they would sound reasonable and understandable to you. However, none of those reasons erases the damage done to my reputation and others' hearts. Reasons don't heal scars. Only God can do that. While I strive to seek forgiveness when I have allowed my emotions to get away with me, there are always consequences.

Moses also faced consequences for his actions. *"But the LORD said to Moses and Aaron, 'Because you did not trust in me enough to honor me as holy in the sight of the Israelites, you will not bring this community into the land I give them'"* (Numbers 20:12). The price of that loss of emotional control was steep. Moses would now never set foot in the Promised Land that he has been leading his people to for all these years. Failure to control emotion can rob us of God's best in our lives and ministry. Moses had every reason to be angry. Miriam has died, and the people did not seem to care enough to give him space to mourn. Suddenly, after 38 years, these people lose faith in Moses and God to provide? After all these years leading these people, Moses doesn't get the benefit of the doubt when things look rough for one hot minute? Moses has every right to be angry, except for the fact that he is a leader. As a leader, he may have the right to be angry, but he never has the right to lose control. This loss of control will cost him the opportunity to lead this nation to its final destination. Joshua will now carry that honor. Moses, in a momentary fit of rage, has forfeited his right to reach the Promised Land.

PLAN SUCCESSION

> *Then Moses went out and spoke these words to all Israel: "I am now a hundred and twenty years old and I am no longer able to lead you. The LORD has said to me, 'You shall not cross the Jordan.' The LORD your God himself will cross over ahead of you. He will destroy these nations before you, and you will take possession of their land."... Then Moses summoned Joshua and said to him in the presence of all Israel, "Be strong and courageous, for you must go with this people into the land that the LORD swore to their ancestors to give them, and you must divide it among them as their inheritance. The LORD himself goes before you and will be with you; he will never leave you nor forsake you. Do not be afraid; do not be discouraged."*
>
> *—Deuteronomy 31:1-3, 7-8*

One of the most important, yet often overlooked, responsibilities of leaders is that of leaving a successor. The Bible reveals God's pattern of working through successive generations.

—Henry and Richard Blackaby, *Spiritual Leadership*

There is a haunting reality that lingers out there in the future of a leader's mind: One day, this will all be over.

And what then? What will become of all we have worked so hard to build? This work that God has called us to, can it possibly be that God's will is to see it diminish and even disappear simply due to lack of next generational leadership? I think not. God intends for us to make a plan for the future of the organization He has empowered us to build. Failure to make a succession plan is failure to actually finish the task. God directed Moses from an early point to keep the young man, Joshua, close to his side. Throughout the story of Moses's life, Joshua has been there. Leading the army into battle, standing watch outside Moses' tent, and even spying out the land when the nation arrived on the shores of the Jordan the first time. This succession plan has been in place a long time, and now it is time to put it into motion. Orderly and successful successions are not an automatic thing. They take time and planning. They take generosity and grace. Leaders must begin early to prepare for that inevitable moment when this will all be over for them.

The Leader's Retirement — Make a Plan

Should God allow us to live long enough, retirement will become a reality for us all. There is a simple truth in life that you just can't fight against — you are getting older. You may be in your teens or twenties as you read this and feel like you can dismiss what I am saying right now, but listen to me. No matter your age now, you are getting older. One day, it's going to catch up with you, but here is the great secret that so many miss: Old age never snuck up on anybody! We all know it's coming.

We just all don't plan for it. Let me encourage you to plan for it. There are two simple things for us to think through when planning for retirement.

Make sure you can afford it

If you haven't started already, get started saving money for retirement. I have heard so many excuses when it comes to not having saved for retirement. Some expect Jesus to return before they retire, so they don't bother saving. They find themselves in a pinch when Jesus doesn't consider their time frame in His universal plan. Some don't think they will ever want to retire, so they just don't plan on it. Then health issues or a change in thinking leaves them wondering what to do next. Some think they will just hit the lottery sometime and retire off of that. Well, that's risky and you really don't want to put your future in the hands of that kind of risk. Ric Edelman asks this question about that kind of thinking when it comes to retirement risk: "Driving from Washington, D.C., to New York City typically takes about four hours. If I drove you there in just 90 minutes, would you reward me for my performance or chastise me for the risk I forced you to take? Methinks you'd chastise me" (Edelman 2016, 91).

Now, I am not simply concerned for the financial security of the retired leader. It goes much deeper than that. A few years ago during a rather dark, emotional period for me, I began to realize that there could come a day that the best thing I could do for the church I have worked to build is get out of the way. If

I ever face one of those dark, emotional periods that just won't go away, I need to leave before I drag the church down with me! But could I afford to do the right thing? I think that it is imperative that pastors and boards of large churches take this retirement question into serious consideration. The last thing my church is going to want is for me to hang on for 10 years too long simply because I cannot afford to retire. The long-term cost of that kind of entrapment would be far more devastating to the organization than the upfront cost of making sure the pastor is prepared for retirement. So, forgive me for falling so squarely into a business and finance place, but old age is not sneaking up on you. You can see it coming from a few decades away! Get ready, because this moment is definitely closer than it seems!

Make sure your organization can survive it

Beyond the simple financial constraints of retirement, there needs to be a clear-eyed consideration of what an organization that can be passed on will look like. In my case, New Life is currently a network of eight different congregations spread out over two states. In the short-term future, we have plans for eight or nine more locally and perhaps expansion into two or three more states. There is a beauty to this method of expanding the Kingdom of God. However, there is also a complexity that will not translate well to a next generation leader. As I look over the network of churches, I realize that it just wouldn't be fair to ask campus pastors, who have signed up to follow the current leadership, to transition to subsequent leadership that they will have no part in choosing. It also wouldn't be fair to ask congregations in various states and counties to submit to a pastor chosen by a distant congregation. Therefore, we are designing the network to fall apart when I am gone. In order to do that, we are making sure our campus pastors, even in video venue campuses, preach on a regular basis. We have done the work of making sure our venues maintain strong and healthy relationships with the denominational structures and districts in which they are physically located. We have made it clear at every level that when Pastor Mike is done, the network will cease to exist. This way, we don't pass on a complex beast that no one knows how to manage. We pass on individual congregations that our districts are already designed to handle. In this way, we ensure that the organization is positioned for the best possible chance for success in the next generation.

The Leader's Encouragement — See Beyond

When I was pastoring in North Carolina, there was an older woman in our church who served on our church board. We were presenting a plan to move forward that was going to cost the church a great deal of money, and much of that money would need to be borrowed money. She was not in favor of getting the church into debt, even though she agreed that the project was the best next move for the congregation. Then one day, I got a call. "Pastor, can I come over and talk to you for a minute?" I replied, "Sure, I will be here in the office." When she arrived, she came in and sat across the desk from me. "Pastor, I'm going to vote for the debt," she declared. Curious as to what I was about to hear, I asked, "Really, what changed your mind?" She said, "I was praying yesterday and God revealed to me that I am worried about debt because I am old. Then He reminded me that His church never gets old. If I were 40 years younger, I would borrow this money and not think twice about it. Since the church isn't old and isn't ever going to be old, I'm going to vote for it!" Wow. At the moment, all I saw was a short-term victory for the agenda I had for the congregation. But I was young then. Now, I see that statement so much more clearly. As I have already said, we have made it clear that when Pastor Mike is done so is the New Life Network of Churches. We don't see that as an ending. We view that as a beginning. It will then be the calling of each of those individual churches to launch new churches and build new networks. The praise report 1,000 years from now in Heaven will be the creation of thousands of networks reaching out to hundreds of thousands of people. I won't be here to see such wild success, but somehow, I will get to be a part of it. Moses, looking out over his people, tells them he is done. Then he begins to paint for them a picture of what their future will look like without him, and he paints a glorious image! God will go before them, God will fight for them, and God will finally give them their Promised Land. Moses can't go any further, but Israel can't be stopped!

The Leader's Endorsement — Pass the Baton

The future leader for Israel will be Joshua. Moses clearly passes the baton to his young protégé. He hands off the reigns of leadership to Joshua without hesitation or reserve. He knows that Joshua will accomplish things that he never did. Moses realizes that Joshua will get the honor of crossing the Jordan. Joshua will get the credit for defeating the formidable inhabitants of Canaan. Joshua will have the privilege of dividing the land among the Israelites and naming cities and towns. He will establish boundaries and build cities. Everything that Moses had dreamed of Joshua will do. Joshua will finally rest in the homeland that Moses never got to establish, and all of that brings joy to the heart of Moses. You might think that Moses would feel resentful, but you would be wrong. For a leader to resent the blessings and honors that will be bestowed on his successor would be so incredibly shortsighted. No, Moses will revel in all that he sees Joshua do. I can see it now. In his mind's eye, Moses looks forward into time and is driven to tears of joy as he sees the people entering the land, Joshua in the lead. Great leaders think like that; they think beyond themselves. "The best leaders lead today with tomorrow in mind by making sure they invest in leaders who will carry their legacy forward. Why? Because a leader's lasting value is measured by succession. That is the Law of Legacy" (Maxwell 2007, 262).

REMEMBER — YOU ARE HEADED TO AN UNMARKED GRAVE

> *Then Moses climbed Mount Nebo from the plains of Moab to the top of Pisgah, across from Jericho. There the LORD showed him the whole land ... Then the LORD said to him, "This is the land I promised on oath to Abraham, Isaac and Jacob when I said, 'I will give it to your descendants.' I have let you see it with your eyes, but you will not cross over into it." And Moses the servant of the LORD died there in Moab, as the LORD had said. He buried him in Moab, in the valley opposite Beth Peor, but to this day no one knows where his grave is.*
>
> *—Deuteronomy 34:1, 4-6*

Of all the things that sustain a leader over time, love is the most lasting. It's hard to imagine leaders getting up day after day, putting in the long hours and hard work it takes to get extraordinary things done, without having their hearts in it. The best-kept secret of successful leaders is love: staying in love with leading, with the people who do the work, with what their organizations produce, and with those who honor the organization by using its products and services. Leadership is not an affair of the head. Leadership is an affair of the heart.

—James M. Kouzes and Barry Z. Posner
The Leadership Challenge

I was sitting in my lonely office in the small church I pastored in 1992. As I rummaged through the desk drawers looking at all the former pastor had left behind, I came across an old directory. It listed every church in the state of North Carolina for a district that no longer existed. Being a bit of a history nerd (and slightly bored), I began looking through the listing of some 80 churches. After a while, I noticed something. There was one name that kept re-emerging as a founding pastor. His last name was Hawkins. He had founded the church I was now the pastor of and a couple of others I had either worked in or attended as a child. I don't know anything about the man, except that he planted all those churches. I don't know his family, his temperament, his education, his skills and abilities, or his frustrations. All I know is that he played a part in my spiritual development. And I am grateful.

Years later, I was sitting in a room filled with leaders of large churches. One of them was seated at the other end of the long table we occupied. His name was Keith Loy. Keith has always amazed me. A man of unending energy and optimism, he had often inspired me by reminding me how slow and sometimes not optimistic I can be. I remember asking him a question once, and I expected some detailed and staged-out plan for an answer. I was amazed when he simply quipped, "I don't know. I just get out of bed every morning and my feet hit the floor trying to figure out how I'm gonna win somebody to Jesus today!" I would love to have that kind of optimism in my mornings. Honestly, until I have some coffee, I'm not even sure I have been won to Jesus most mornings! I guess that optimism is why I was so shocked by what he said at that table. In the midst of a conversation about legacy or church growth or something like that, he just said, "You know, one day I'm headed to an unmarked grave." Well, I had never seen it that way before. I have always realized that no one is going to remember who I am in a generation or two, but that idea of an unmarked grave seemed so dark, so unfair.

But he is right.

And that is how it should be.

I have often given thought to why God would bury Moses Himself and then not tell anyone where he was buried. These days, it makes sense to me. Had the Israelites had the bones of Moses, they just might have put them somewhere to revere them. Over time, that reverence might have turned to worship. Worship of the creature instead of the Creator would have been the greatest insult that could have ever been levied on the legacy of Moses. And so, God protected him. Moses had not served perfectly, but he had served brilliantly. His mistakes made him into a man who could lead and a man from which we could learn. Moses' imperfection is such a wonderful encouragement for us. Knowing we don't have to be perfect to be used is freeing and empowering. Knowing that God is not surprised by our weaknesses is comforting. "People, because we are people, will make mistakes in the process of fulfilling our potential. God both expects those mistakes and is prepared to tolerate them, as long as they are stepping stones in our individual paths to greatness" (Grumet 2014, 229). In an unmarked grave somewhere just outside of the Promised Land, the bones of Moses still lay.

But his work continues.

Moses left behind the Law of the Israelites that still animates the lives of Jews and Christians to this day. Moses left behind commandments and histories that still teach to this day. But mostly, Moses left behind a people who found a land that was promised to them by the God of Heaven. Those people are back there today. The people of Israel are the legacy of Moses. Those people would have simply become a subset of Egyptians. Instead, they stood from the day Moses brought them out of Egypt to this very day as a testament to the greatness of God who called them His people before they ever were a people. He called them His nation when they were but one family. Moses, by leading them out of their bondage and into their promise, leaves a legacy that lasts to this day. "Our ability as leaders will not be measured by the buildings we built, the institutions we established, or what our team accomplished during our tenure. You and I will be judged by how well the people we invested in carried on after we are gone" (Maxwell 2007, 263-264).

Let me encourage you. Live. Live every minute with the enthusiasm of a small child entering a toy store. Life is incredible, and there is so much to do and see. Go do it. Go see it. Live.

Let me encourage you. Lead. Lead every chance you get through the power and guidance of the Holy Spirit. Life is too precious to waste by not investing in others. Lead people and make their lives better.

Let me encourage you. Leave something beautiful behind. I have built congregations, buildings, staff teams, structures, events, and services. I have built many things in my life. But none of that will last. No one will remember the services or staff structures. There may come a day when the congregations dwindle and the buildings sit empty. All over the world, there will be people. People who will never know my name but whose lives have somehow been touched by people God gave me the honor of impacting for His glory. He does it. He will be praised. He will be glorified. I will be forgotten. But, oh, the honor of having influenced people! That's what He cares about ... people.

If leadership is influence ... and influence can help people ... and He cares about people ... and I get to influence them ... yeah, that makes it all worthwhile.

REFERENCES

Addison, Steve. 2011. *Movements That Change The World*. Downers Grove, Illinois: InterVarsity Press.

Blackaby, Henry and Richard. 2008. *Experiencing God*. Nashville, Tennessee: B&H Publishing Group.

Blackaby, Henry and Richard. 2001. *Spiritual Leadership*. Nashville, Tennessee: Broadman & Holman Publishers.

Clinton, Dr. J. Robert. 1988. *The Making of a Leader*. Colorado Springs, Colorado: NavPress.

Cohen, Norman J. 2007. *Moses and the Journey to Leadership*. Woodstock, Vermont: Jewish Lights Publishing.

Collins, Jim. 2001. *Good To Great*. New York, New York: HarperCollins Publishers Inc.

Collins, Jim. 2009. *How The Mighty Fall*. New York, New York: HarperCollins Publishers Inc.

Collins, Jim and Jerry I. Porras. 2002. *Built To Last*. New York, New York: HarperCollins Publishers.

Crouch, Andy. 2016. *Strong and Weak*. Downers Grove, Illinois: InterVarsity Press.

Dilenschneider, Robert L. 2000. *Moses: CEO*. Beverly Hills, California: New Millennium Press.

Edelman, Ric. 2016. *Rescue Your Money*. New York, New York: Simon & Schuster Paperbacks.

Goleman, Daniel, Richard Boyatzis, and Annie McKee. 2013. *Primal Leadership*. Boston, Massachusetts: Harvard Business Review Press.

Grumet, Zvi. 2014. *Moses and the Path to Leadership.* Jerusalem, New York: Urim Publications.

Kotter, John P. and Dan S. Cohen. 2002. *The Heart of Change.* Boston, Massachusetts: Harvard Business Review Press.

Kouzes, James M. and Barry Z. Posner. 2012. *The Leadership Challenge.* San Francisco, California: The Leadership Challenge.

Lencioni, Patrick. 2012. *The Advantage.* San Francisco, California: Jossey-Bass.

Lencioni, Patrick. 2002. *The Five Dysfunctions of a Team.* San Francisco, California: Jossey-Bass.

Lennox, Stephen J. 2016. *Moses: Faithful Servant of God.* Indianapolis, Indiana: Wesleyan Publishing House.

Lewis, Jacqueline J. 2008. *The Power of Stories.* Nashville, Tennessee: Abingdon Press.

Maxwell, John C. 2010. *Everyone Communicates, Few Connect.* Nashville, Tennessee: Thomas Nelson, Inc.

Maxwell, John C. 2001. *The 17 Indisputable Laws of Teamwork.* Nashville, Tennessee: Thomas Nelson, Inc.

Maxwell, John C. 2007. *The 21 Irrefutable Laws of Leadership.* Nashville, Tennessee: Thomas Nelson, Inc.

Northouse, Peter G. 2010. *Leadership Theory and Practice.* Los Angeles, California: Sage Publications, Inc.

Nouwen, Henri J. M. 1989. *In the Name of Jesus.* New York, New York: The Crossroad Publishing Company.

Petersen, Bruce L., Edward A. Thomas, and Bob Whitesel. 2010. *Foundations of Church Administration.* Kansas City, Kansas: Beacon Hill Press.

Reiland, Dan. 2011. *Amplified Leadership.* Lake Mary, Florida: Charisma House.

Roxburgh, Alan J. and Fred Romanuk. 2006. *The Missional Leader.* San Francisco, California: Jossey-Bass.

Schmidt, Wayne. 2006. *Power Plays.* Indianapolis, Indiana: Wesleyan Publishing House.

Schmidt, Wayne. 2017. *Surrender.* Indianapolis, Indiana: Wesleyan Publishing House.

Sinek, Simon. 2014. *Leaders Eat Last.* New York, New York: Penguin Group.

Smith, Mark and David W. Wright. 2011. *The Church Leader's MBA.* Circleville, Ohio: Ohio Christian University Press.

Stanley, Andy, Reggie Joiner, and Lane Jones. 2004. *7 Practices of Effective Ministry.* Colorado Springs, Colorado: Multnomah Books.

Willink, Jocko and Leif Babin. 2015. *Extreme Ownership.* New York, New York: St. Martin's Press.

Wright, N.T. 2015. *Simply Good News.* New York, New York: HarperCollins Publishers.

All Scripture quotations are taken from *The Holy Bible,* New International Version.

ABOUT THE AUTHOR

Mike Hilson is the Senior Pastor of New Life Church based in La Plata, Maryland. Since 1999, the church has grown under his leadership from a congregation of less than 100 attendees into several churches and video venues. The New Life Network of churches now averages more than 5,000 in regular attendance across Maryland and Northern Virginia.

Mike currently serves on the Board of Trustees at Southern Wesleyan University. He also is a member of the Chesapeake District Board of Administration as well as the General Board of Administration of the Wesleyan Church. He lives in the D.C. Metro Area with his wife, Tina. They have three sons, Robert, Stephen, and Joshua, who have taken this journey of ministry with them.

Books by Mike Hilson include *Napkin Theology*, *Speak Life*, *A Significant Impact for Christ*, and a series of books called *Coffee with the Pastor*.